Making Classroom Assessment Work

Fourth Edition

Making Classroom Assessment Work

Fourth Edition

Anne Davies, Ph.D.

CONNECT2LEARNING

Printed and bound in Canada by Hignell Book Printing.
22 21 20   5 4 3 2

Project Manager: Judith Hall-Patch
Design: Beachwalker Studio, Ken Chong, Tom Collver, Mackenzie Duncan, Cori Jones

Library and Archives Canada Cataloguing in Publication

Title: Making classroom assessment work / Anne Davies.
Name: Davies, Anne, 1955- author.
Description: Fourth edition.
Identifiers: Canadiana 20190128836 | ISBN 9781928092070 (softcover)
Subjects: LCSH: Educational tests and measurements.
Classification: LCC LB3051 .D38 2020 | DDC 371.26—dc23

CONNECT2LEARNING
2449D Rosewall Crescent
Courtenay, BC V9N 8R9
CANADA
1-800-603-9888 (North America only)
1-250-703-2920
1-250-703-2921 (Fax)
books@connect2learning.com
www.connect2learning.com

Discounts available on bulk orders.

Contents

In memory of my children's grandparents

Patricia Davies
1923 – 1993

William Davies
1920 – 2006

Blanche Duncan
1920 – 1999

James Duncan
1916 – 2009

With appreciation for their love and support

Preface

Research has shown that involving students in classroom assessment results in considerable gains in achievement, "amongst the largest ever reported for educational interventions" (Black and Wiliam, 1998). Over the past decades, because of this and similar research findings, educators are seeking new methods to help them verify where students are on their learning journey and to give them the information they need to take their next steps. This book is designed to provide educators and students with a framework to use assessment in the service of learning.

Before setting out to reach their goals via an unfamiliar path, seasoned adventurers prepare themselves by seeking out the tools and gear needed to make the trip a success. Hikers know the importance of good boots in providing them with secure footing, solid support, safety and protection on the trail, as well as the comfort they need to keep on going to the end.

Assessment *for* learning provides a strong foundation for teachers to work with their students in planning and carrying out quality classroom assessment. These methods, like good hiking boots, will support learners and give them a sound footing for their lifelong learning journey. By participating in the assessment process, students experience safety in knowing what to expect on the road, and comfort and security in the recognition of their own achievement. As well, using assessment to actively engage students means everyone is more likely to enjoy the learning journey.

Making Classroom Assessment Work offers ideas to be explored and adapted. This book is designed to deepen understanding of classroom assessment, through reading and through application of the ideas found in the *Guiding Your Own Learning* activities at the end of each chapter. As well, questions in each chapter help teachers identify key decision points in planning their own individual strategies and carrying out assessment *for* learning in a way that fits their classrooms. And, explicit next steps to use with students help teachers move beyond consideration of big ideas to implementation. Making these thoughtful decisions and selecting first steps is the key to success. In this new edition, I have revisited the research studies which underlie this work as well as updating the context of student learning and changes in technology.

Making Classroom Assessment Work

***"An event is not an experience until you reflect upon it."*

Michael Fullan

An important first step for making classroom assessment work is to understand the difference between assessment and evaluation. The terms *assessment* and *evaluation* are sometimes used interchangeably, but they have different meanings. When teachers assess, they gather information about student learning to inform teaching so students learn more. Teachers may teach differently, based on what they find as they assess student learning. When teachers evaluate, they decide whether or not students have learned what they needed to learn. They collect evidence to verify how well students have learned it. Evaluation is a process of reviewing the evidence and determining its value. To illustrate the difference, consider the following scenario:

> Three students are taking a course in how to pack a parachute. Imagine that the class average is represented by a dotted line. Student Number One initially scored very high, but his scores have dropped as the end of the course approaches. Student Number Two's evaluations are erratic. Sometimes he does very well and sometimes he doesn't. The teacher has a hard time predicting from day to day how he will do. Student Number Three did very poorly in relation to the class for the first two-thirds of the course, but has lately figured out how to successfully pack a parachute.

Which of these students would you want to pack your parachute? Number One? Number Two? Number Three? Most people would choose Number Three. The problem is that Number Three did not

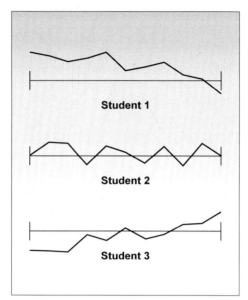

Student 1

Student 2

Student 3

pass the course. When his grades were tallied and averaged, they weren't high enough. Number One and Number Two did pass.

This scenario highlights a key question teachers need to address before taking action. When should teachers assess and when should they evaluate? What might be the results of evaluating too early or too much? How do teachers know if they are evaluating the right things? How do teachers know what makes sense for the learner and for the course?

Expert teachers are careful to give students time to learn. When students are acquiring new skills, knowledge, and understanding, they need a chance to practice. Assessment supports learning when teachers use it to:

- check to see what has been learned and what needs to be learned next
- access and give students specific and descriptive feedback in relation to criteria that is focused on improvement
- involve students in assessment – the person most able to improve the learning

Assessment is used to collect information that will inform the teacher's next teaching steps and the student's next learning steps. In some jurisdictions - provinces, states, territories, countries - this process is referred to as Assessment *for* Learning. Other jurisdictions use Assessment for learning to refer to teachers using formative assessment to inform their teaching and Assessment *as* learning to refer to students learning to engage in metacognition – to self-monitor their way to success. Whatever terms your jurisdiction uses, it's important to ask "Does this support student learning?" If so, no matter what labels might be used, chances are you are using assessment in the service of learning.

Assessment *for* learning involves learners receiving a considerable amount of *descriptive* feedback during their learning. Descriptive feedback gives information that enables the learner to adjust what he or she is doing in order to improve (Gibbs and Stobart 1993; Hattie and Timperley 2007).

Descriptive feedback comes from many sources, such as teachers, peers, and the students themselves, as they compare their work to samples and related criteria. Feedback may take the form of specific comments about the work, information such as posted criteria that describe quality, or models and exemplars that show what quality can look like.

Evaluation is different. It tells the learner how she or he has performed as compared to others or to some standard. When teachers evaluate, they consider the evidence of learning available and decide whether or not students have learned what was needed, and how well they have learned it. Evaluation is often reported using grades, numbers, checks, or other symbols – it is encoded. Evaluation and evaluative feedback are often labelled assessment *of* learning.

Research Connection:

Involving students in assessment and increasing the amount of descriptive feedback, while decreasing evaluative feedback, increases student learning significantly. While all students show gains, students who usually achieve the least show the largest gains overall. (Black and Wiliam 1998: Harlen 2006; Hayward et al. 2015; Hill et al. 2017)

Many classroom teachers have experienced the negative effects on learning and relationships with students when they evaluate before students have had time to learn. Research confirms the finding that if teachers evaluate too early they limit descriptive feedback and risk interrupting the learning. When teachers assess during the learning and evaluate at the end of the learning, they give students time to practice and improve before judging the evidence.

When engaged in assessment *of* learning, teachers are checking to see what has been learned to date. This professional judgment and the evaluation that results is often summarized into scores or grades. This is called assessment *of* learning or evaluation. At the classroom level, assessment *of* learning information is used to communicate progress toward standards to students, parents, and other educators. At the school, district, or system level, evaluation information is used in a variety of ways to inform the school, district, or system's next steps in supporting student learning through action.

A Classroom Assessment Process That Works

There are three general parts to a classroom assessment process that works. First, teachers review the curriculum and standards documents and describe for themselves the learning that students are expected to accomplish. They collect and review samples and models that show what the learning looks like for students of a particular age range, and they think through the kinds of evidence their students could produce to show they have mastered what they needed to learn (Herbst and Davies, 2016).

Second, when the big picture is established, teachers work with students to bring them into the assessment process. They do this by talking about the learning, showing samples and discussing what the evidence might look like, and setting criteria with students. Students then engage in activities such as self-assessment, peer assessment, goal setting, and collecting evidence of their learning to deepen their understanding. They present their work to others and receive more feedback. This cycle continues as students are involved in resetting criteria and continuing their learning. As students participate in assessment, they become partners in the continuous assessment *for* learning cycle.

Third, teachers evaluate; they 'sum up' the learning (summative evaluation). At this time, they look at all the evidence of learning collected by students and by the teacher from multiple sources over time, and make a judgment regarding the degree to which students have learned what they need to learn (Herbst and Davies 2016).

Research Connection:

When students are involved in their own assessment, mistakes become feedback they can use to adjust what they are doing. When students' mistakes are identified by others and feedback is limited to grades or scores, students are less likely to know what to do differently next time. (Andrade 2011; Brookhart 2001; Butler 1987; Shepard 2000)

Seeing it work

What does this process look like in a classroom? The rest of this chapter presents an example of what assessment and instruction can look like. In this example, students are learning how to conduct a research project.

We are going to be working on a research project over the next few weeks. It is important for you to learn how to gather information and make sense of it for yourself and for your life. Think about the Internet. There is a lot of information available, but for it to be of any use, you have to decide what you want to know, make choices about what information to take seriously and what to ignore, and then decide what it all means for you. That's being a critical thinker – a thoughtful user of information. So, what do you think is important about engaging in a research project?

When students are engaged in thoughtful, focused conversation about any learning activity or task beforehand, the talk clarifies options, highlights possible plans, and encourages sharing of information with others. As students work with teachers to define what learning is and what it looks like, they shift from being passive learners to being actively involved in their own learning. By being engaged, they use and build more neural pathways in their brains. This means they are more likely to be able to access their learning more easily and for a longer period of time – far beyond the end of the unit or test.

When teachers talk about what is to be learned, why it is relevant to students' lives, and then invite students to define what it might look like once they've learned it, students begin to understand what needs to be learned. They have a chance to prepare to learn. Many learning theorists propose that we interpret the world through our mental models – that is, we see what we expect to see and hear what we expect to hear. Emerging work in neuroscience supports this perspective (Brabeck 2008; Restak 2003). When students are involved in assessment from the beginning, they are more ready to learn. When we involve students they are more likely to:

- understand what is expected of them
- access prior knowledge
- have ownership and engagement in the learning process
- be able to give themselves descriptive feedback as they are learning
- give information that teachers need to adjust their teaching

Knowing what they are learning and what it looks like, gives students the information they need to assess *themselves* as they learn – to keep themselves on track. Learning to self-monitor in this way is an essential skill for independent, self-directed, lifelong learners. It leads to self-regulation, co-regulation, and improves executive functioning (Andrade, 2011; Allal, 2014).

Showing Samples and Discussing the Evidence

I am going to give you several examples of research projects. Here are weblinks, posters, videos, booklets, and timelines. I want you to work in groups to analyze these student projects. Think about what is really important in a research project. Especially think about how information is effectively communicated. When you are ready, we will list your ideas and create criteria for our research project. We can record the criteria on a T-chart so you can refer to it as you work.

When we give students samples to review, and when we talk with them about what is important in their learning, we help them build mental models of what success looks like. This is particularly important for the students who struggle the most.

When teachers spend time with students, sharing samples as well as connecting what students already know to what they need to know, it increases students' understanding of what they will be learning and of what will be assessed. This helps them use their prior knowledge and learn the language of learning and assessment.

Be careful when choosing samples to show students. If samples are limited to showing what students already know and can do, they fail to orient students towards what they need to know next. When samples represent work that is too far away from what students know and are able to do, students may not see how to get from where they are to where they need to be. And the more our students learn to represent learning in different ways, the more prepared they are for this rapidly changing world.

Getting on with the learning

It's time for you to get started on your research projects. We are going to begin with a small quick one so you can all practice with the support of a group before you do a larger research project independently. This is also a chance for you to find out what you already know about doing a research project and a chance to learn from your group members.

For this first project, I would like you to work in small groups. I want your group to choose something you are interested in learning more about.

Choose something where the information will be easy to find, since you will only have a week to do this research project. Perhaps it will be something you already know a lot about, such as a sport, music, an issue, or pets. Think of topics that interest you and your classmates. In a week's time, your group will make a presentation to the class. At that time, we will be using the criteria we created to assess your work. Keep it in mind as you are working.

Giving students time to discover what they already know and to learn from each other provides a scaffold for future learning. When conversations about learning take place in the group, learners can check their thinking and performance and develop deeper understanding of their learning. Researchers studying the role of emotions and the brain say that experiences such as these prepare learners to take the risks necessary for learning (Alexander 2001; Michaels et al. 2008; Pert 1999).

Doing things more than once is also essential for learning. It is when students do something the second and third time that they come to understand what they know and what they need to know. Students need practice time to learn. Through repetition, they are able to take what they are learning and apply it at deeper and deeper levels.

Practicing

Class, you've had a week to work on your draft research projects. Tomorrow you'll be presenting the work you've done so far to members of the class. Please sign up if you want your presentation recorded on video. It will be your decision whether or not to include the video in your portfolio.

Remember our purpose. This is a chance for you to find out what you already knew about doing a research project, as well as to learn from your group members. Remember, we are going to use the criteria we agreed on to assess your work. At this time, there will be detailed feedback to improve your work. No grades will be given.

After you do your presentations, I will ask your peers to post comments in relation to the criteria on Google Docs. Each group has opened an online feedback forum. I will also be using the criteria we developed to give specific feedback to help improve the presentations. Any questions?

Some students seem to know what teachers want without it having to be explained in detail. It seems others simply don't get it. When teachers make the criteria explicit, share the process of learning, and give descriptive feedback according to the agreed-upon criteria, they give more students the opportunity to learn. They begin to make more of the implicit expectations explicit.

When teachers give students a chance to share their knowledge with each other and with their teachers, they learn and teachers learn. Celebrating one's accomplishments by sharing work with others is part of the learning process. The audience can be made up of classmates, other classes, parents and guardians, or community members. They may be present to one another directly or via email or the Internet. When the learning is captured in print or in digital form, it becomes concrete evidence that can be used later for student conferences and in reports to others.

Self-Assessment

> As you think about your work, I want you to review the criteria we set together (see example on page 56). Take a few moments and write in your journal the things that you noticed you were able to do well and two things you need to work on next.

When students and teachers self-assess, they confirm, consolidate, and integrate new knowledge. Debriefing after the learning provides an opportunity for collaborative feedback – from student and teacher perspectives. *What do we think we learned? What worked? What didn't? What might we do differently next time?*

When students self-assess, they gain insights that help them monitor their learning, as well as practice in giving themselves descriptive feedback. When student self-assessments are shared with teachers, teachers gain a better understanding about where students are in relation to where they need to be.

Research Connection:

Self-assessment asks students to make choices about what to focus on next in their learning. When students make choices about their learning, achievement increases; when choice is absent, learning decreases. (Boud 2003; Gearhart and Wolf 1995; Harlen 2006; Harlen and Deakin-Crick 2003)

Revisiting Criteria

Now that you have completed the research project and a draft presentation, it is time to revisit the criteria we set. I noticed that some groups did things which the audience found informative and effective, yet those weren't part of the criteria on our T-chart. Your presentations and projects may have reminded you of other things that make a research project powerful. Does anyone have any ideas about what needs to be added, changed, or taken away?

As students learn and assess, they define and redefine the criteria. Over time, the criteria become increasingly more specific, as students discover how to apply their learning, hone their process skills, and produce high-quality work. It is important that the criteria allow for the many different ways students may select to represent the results of their research. For example, when carefully constructed, the same criteria can be used effectively for a timeline, a poster, a written project, or a model. Using criteria that allow for a range of representation encourages students to represent what they know in a variety of ways, and enables teachers to fairly assess a variety of projects.

Feedback to Forward the Learning

When students self-assess in relation to criteria or samples of student work, they are giving themselves feedback that is explicit and provides clear direction. Because the feedback takes place in the context of explicit criteria, which students have helped to set, it is more likely students will understand what needs to be done differently next time. Explicit criteria and samples of student work help increase the possibility that when students interact with an audience – peers, parents, teachers, and others – and receive specific feedback, in relation to criteria, the next steps in their learning will be more informed.

Consider the teacher who tries to give students a lot of timely feedback. Over the course of a week, she or he works hard and manages to give each student specific, descriptive feedback four times.

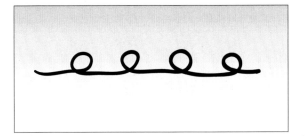

Now imagine the teacher has involved students in co-constructing criteria. Before asking students to turn in their work for feedback, she pauses and asks students to self-assess using criteria that they have developed together (i.e., give

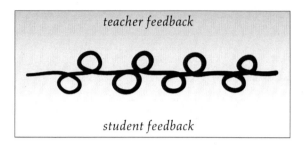

teacher feedback

student feedback

themselves feedback). Without the teacher working any harder, the students receive twice the amount of feedback to feed their learning forward.

Then imagine the classroom is a place where everyone understands quality because they have set criteria together after examining samples and have been using the language of assessment with each other. This time the teacher asks students to give their work to someone else to assess, using the

criteria. Their job is to review the work and find evidence of two things that meet the criteria and to select one thing from the agreed-upon criteria list that needs to be improved.

Next, students are asked to self-assess and give themselves specific, descriptive feedback. The teacher receives the work and gives the students specific, descriptive feedback that also feeds the learning forward.

Now let's go further. What about the classroom where every student has access to a device? Could students post their work in an online forum or send their work to people in other places and get even more feedback to forward the learning? Absolutely. Research shows that students seek feedback when it is easily available and when their work can be improved (Davies 2004; Hattie 2007; Wiliam et al. 2004).

Setting goals

> Please look at the criteria and your self-assessment, and think about what you need to focus on in the future. This will become your goal. It is part of preparing for next week's new project. Do not take on too many things – one or two goals are about all anyone can handle. Record one or two goals, what your first steps are going to be, and who you are going to partner with for support.

When students work together to look at samples, set criteria, self-assess, and reset criteria, they come to understand the process of assessment and they practice using the language of assessment. Through this process, students gain a clear picture of what they need to learn and where they are in relation to where they need to be, making it possible for them to begin to identify next steps in their learning. Setting goals is a powerful way to focus students' learning. Using this process is an indication of teachers moving from being effective to expert (Hattie and Timperley 2007).

Ongoing Assessment *for* Learning

> Class, before you leave today, I'd like you to post on the online forum. Record two things you've learned about research projects so far and one question you have. Thank you.

When we think about what we've done, we may come to understand it in a different way. Self-assessment gives learners the opportunity to think about their thinking and their learning – a process called *metacognition*. Students who are able to self-assess – that is, to reflect on how they learn – are better able to monitor their own learning process. These approaches may be particularly important for children and young people who do not have extra support for learning outside the classroom. When students share their thinking with teachers, students learn more and teachers can teach better.

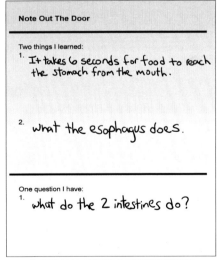

Note Out The Door

Two things I learned:
1. It takes 6 seconds for food to reach the stomach from the mouth.

2. what the esophagus does.

One question I have:
1. what do the 2 intestines do?

Available as a reproducible at connect2learning.com

Sharing the work

Linking assessment and learning in deliberate intentional ways helps students come to know the *process* of learning as much as the learning content itself. Involving students in their own assessment leads to greater student ownership and investment in the learning than when the responsibility for assessment (and for learning) rests entirely with the teacher.

As students become more involved in the assessment process, teachers find themselves working differently. They used to be solely responsible for providing information about the learning. Now there are as many references for students to use as there are models, exemplars, samples, posted criteria, and peers. Many teachers are spending less time grading at the end of the learning and more time helping students during the learning. As teachers find more ways to involve students and increase the amount of descriptive feedback, while decreasing the evaluative feedback, they are discovering for themselves what Black and Wiliam (1998) found in their research – students are learning more.

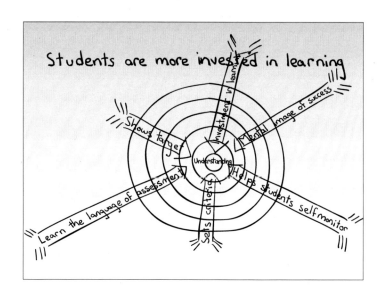

Research Connection:

When students are involved in their own assessment, they are required to think about their learning and articulate their understanding – which helps them learn. (Black and Wiliam 2009; Boud 2000; Hill et al. 2017)

Rethinking

Thanks to research and theory concerning learning, intelligence, the brain, the role of emotions, and what it means to be a self-directed learner, we are rethinking the role of classroom assessment in supporting student learning. As we see ways to make classroom assessment work, we are asking how we can:

- build a foundation for assessment in our classrooms (Chapter 2)
- help students understand what they are to learn (Chapter 3)
- use samples to show what the learning could look like (Chapter 4)
- decide what counts as evidence (Chapter 5)
- involve students in classroom assessment (Chapter 6)
- make assessment-learning connections from primary to post-secondary (Chapter 7)
- involve students in collecting, organizing, and presenting evidence (Chapter 8)
- involve students in communicating about learning (Chapter 9)
- explore student-parent-teacher conferences; consider professional judgment, evaluation, and reporting (Chapter 10)
- deepen our own understanding and the understanding of others about classroom assessment (Chapter 11)

As you work with the research-based classroom assessment practices in this book, consider yourself invited to develop your own expertise in the area of classroom assessment. As you consider the issues, become more familiar with the research, make your plans, and work with students and colleagues, you will find your own ways to make classroom assessment work better for you and for your students. The journey to better quality classroom assessment is too important to miss.

" *We don't receive wisdom; we must discover it for ourselves after a journey that no one can take for us or spare us.* **"**
Marcel Proust

Guiding Our Own Learning

You already know some things about classroom assessment. I invite you to think about what you would like to add to your assessment practices and what you might like to stop doing, so you have time to do the new thing well.

1. Begin by thinking about what you have read so far. *Has it confirmed some things for you? Did you realize you were already doing some of this? Did it remind you of anything you had forgotten?*
2. Record something you would like to learn more about. Talk with someone else about your thinking.

Guiding the Learning of Students

As you prepare students to assess their way to success, consider asking them about assessment. Pose questions, such as:
- What is the best way to show what you know?
- How do you learn best?
- What helps you remember?
- What kind of feedback helps your learning?
- Do you like to learn and practice by yourself or with others?

Listening to learners informs our teaching practice.

Building the Foundation for Classroom Assessment

"Every discovery of what is false leads us to seek earnestly after what is true, and every fresh experience points out some form of error, which we shall afterward carefully avoid.

John Keats

Building a classroom environment that supports learning involves finding out who your students are, letting them find out who you are, and establishing classroom agreements about how everyone will work and learn together.

In order to fully participate in their learning and assessment, students need a safe school environment in which to learn. This includes a classroom community of learners where students know what matters and learn ways to get along with others. When we create a classroom community that is safe for learners, they are more likely to take risks necessary for learning. This type of community develops when learners know how to *give* help, how to *get* help, what help to get, and how to use the help to improve their learning.

Students and teachers can be engaged in assessment *for* learning when everyone:
- knows that mistakes are essential for learning
- understands how to give and receive feedback
- takes time to learn
- recognizes that success has many different looks

Mistakes are Essential for Learning

Learning involves taking risks and making mistakes, and then doing things differently as a result. Mistakes provide assessment evidence – they give learners feedback about what is not working and bring them closer to knowing what will work. Unless students understand that mistakes are essential for learning, they may not take the risks necessary for it to occur.

Many years ago, educational theorist John Dewey (1933) referred to learning and reflecting on the learning (self-assessment) as a continuous cycle – a *learning loop:* we learn, we assess, we learn some more. Now, many years later, brain research is again pointing to the critical need for self-assessment in all learning. Current research affirms the brain is *self-referencing;* that is, we decide what to do next based on an assessment of what we have just done.

When teachers deliberately model making mistakes and fixing them, students learn to value their own mistakes as a source of information for their learning, and as feedback indicating what they need to do differently. Knowing both what to do and what not to do can help learners understand what choices to make to support learning.

Understanding Feedback

Learners understand feedback. It is what they get when they try to shoot a basket and make it or don't make it. It is what happens when someone laughs as they share a funny story. It is what the teacher gives when students finish an assignment or turn in their homework. What students don't usually understand is that there are different types of feedback – descriptive feedback and evaluative feedback.

Descriptive feedback for learning

Feedback for learning – specific, descriptive feedback – tells students about their learning. They find out what is working ("do more of this") and what is not ("do less of this"). They can use this information to adjust what they're doing to become more successful and to learn from their mistakes.

Since many teachers find it difficult to give students enough descriptive feedback, they make available other sources of reference for them, such as posted samples or criteria created with students. Students can also give themselves descriptive feedback when they compare their work to models, posted samples, or detailed criteria. They also receive descriptive feedback when their classmates use criteria to describe one specific thing that met the criteria and one question they have (see example on this page).

Descriptive feedback gives the learner information about their learning that helps them self-reference and plan their next steps. This type of feedback:

- comes during, as well as after, the learning
- is easily understood and relates directly to the learning
- is specific, so performance can improve
- involves choice on the part of the learner as to the type of feedback and how to receive it
- is part of an ongoing conversation about the learning
- is in comparison to models, exemplars, samples, or descriptions
- is about the performance or the work – not the person

Example of Descriptive Feedback

Criteria for MAP	Sample Match
- EASY TO READ AND FIND THE PLACES	Closest match is sample # 2 because...
	- IT'S EASY TO READ
- LOCATIONS ARE ACCURATELY LABELLED/ PLACED	- YOU MISPLACED THE DANUBE RIVER
- NOTHING IS MISSING	- YOU MISSED THE ATLANTIC OCEAN
Conference requested ☐	Question(s):
Date(s) received: OCT. 1	
Assessed by ☑ teacher ☐ self ☐ partner ☐ other	Assignment: MAP #3 EUROPE Student: JAMIE G, BLOCK E

Adapted from Gregory, Cameron, and Davies, *Setting and Using Criteria*, 2nd Edition, 43.

Evaluative feedback tells the learner how she or he has performed as compared to others (norm-referenced assessment) or as compared to what was to be learned (criterion-referenced assessment). Evaluative feedback is often reported using grades, numbers, checks, or other symbols. Because evaluative feedback has been encoded into a summary comment ("great job") or a symbol of some kind (B, 72%, 3), students usually understand whether or not they need to improve but not *how* to improve.

Unless specific, descriptive feedback is also provided, students may not have enough information to understand what they need to do in order to improve. When evaluative feedback is present, struggling students may not attend to the descriptive feedback (Butler 1988; Shute 2008). Successful students seem better able to decode the evaluative feedback and use the information to support their learning (Brookhart 2001).

Research shows that evaluative feedback can interrupt many students' learning (Black and Wiliam 1998; Butler 1987, 1988; Hattie 2008; Hattie and Timperley 2007). When students understand what needs to be learned and are involved in gathering evidence of their learning, it is easier for them to see evaluation as part of the learning process, rather than as a defining moment describing success or failure. Teachers seeking to improve student learning are advised to *reduce* the amount of evaluative feedback and *increase* the amount of descriptive feedback during learning and practice time.

Research Connection:

Current feedback research is finding that the feedback that best supports student learning is specific and descriptive. It tells students what to do more of and what to do less of. Evaluative feedback, such as grades, scores, or other encoded information can interfere with student learning. (Black and Wiliam 2018, 1998; Butler 1988, 1987; Hattie and Timperley 2007; Shute 2008; Wiliam et al. 2004)

Time to Learn

In order to learn, students need time to process. This is because meaning (learning) is only generated from within (Jensen 1998). When we have more time to think about our learning, we learn more. Since teachers are pressured with the demands of curriculum expectations, they may not give students time to do the processing they need in order to learn. When students are encouraged to talk about their learning and to self-assess in relation to criteria, models, or exemplars, they are giving themselves descriptive feedback that helps them learn more. It is also a way teachers can give structured processing time.

People used to picture learning as students sitting quietly and listening. That is only a small part of what needs to happen for learning to take place. Students need to construct their understandings in interaction with self, others, and their environment (Bruner 1986; Perrenoud 1998; Vygotsky 1978). Learning takes time because it involves interaction and processing. Teachers are realizing that when they slow down and engage students, students are more likely to understand what they are to learn and what quality looks like. When students have time to think about their learning and decide what needs to be changed or improved, they can set goals. This is an example of assessment in the service of learning.

Students need time to:

- set and use criteria
- self-assess
- receive and give descriptive feedback
- collect proof or evidence of learning
- set and reset their goals
- seek specific support for their learning
- communicate their learning to others

These are examples of processing time. It takes time to involve students in their learning and in the assessment process. Start slowly. Students will believe we value their words and their contributions when they see, hear, and experience us appreciating them.

Research Connection:

Co-constructing criteria changes the teaching and learning environment. Having criteria results in more students being engaged and learning at higher levels. (Black and Wiliam 2018; Joslin 2002; Young 2000)

Success Has Different Looks

Students have a better chance of being successful if they know what success looks like. For example, we cannot assume that students know what a good presentation or retelling looks like unless they have witnessed one. There is too much room for miscommunication when we use only words to describe quality.

There are many ways to help students understand and recognize success. We can demonstrate a process and ask students to analyze and identify the steps. As we do so, we deliberately model metacognitive talk by sharing the details of our thinking out loud. We can invite those who have knowledge or ideas to demonstrate what something means or might look like. We can bring in guests to perform (such as another class who has already been practicing a particular skill), watch videos of other classes, or look at student work from previous years. These all give reference points, models, and exemplars to support learning.

Students also need access to a range of samples of what success looks like along the way, such as, three different writing samples showing development in paragraph construction over time, or four different ways students presented their research findings in previous years. Showing students a range of samples conveys the message that their job, no matter where they are in their learning, is to improve by learning more. By doing so, teachers acknowledge for students that learning is a continuous process and that everyone learns in different ways and at different rates. If we present learning as something that all students do in the same way at the same time, we may create hopelessness in those students who don't understand how to improve or how to demonstrate their knowledge. By not helping students to picture success, we jeopardize their learning.

We also need to invite students to think about different ways they could show proof that they have learned something. By allowing for different learning styles and different ways of representing what has been learned, we increase the opportunities for students to use all of their knowledge, skills, and experience.

Together, through conversations and looking at samples, students and teachers can define the many looks of success. By discussing what something looks and sounds like, they build a shared vocabulary – a shared language for assessment. Students can use the language of assessment to self-assess and manage their own learning. Without this shared language and vision of success, students may not understand, use, or be assisted in their learning through the classroom assessment process.

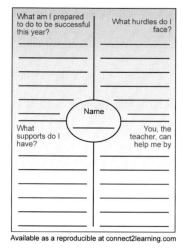

Available as a reproducible at connect2learning.com

Involving Parents

Part of the foundation for classroom assessment is effective communication with parents and others who support students' learning. Teachers build relationships that extend beyond the classroom through invitations to share information, goal setting conferences, and checking in. The sooner we begin, the better.

Invitations to share

Many teachers email, text, or telephone parents. They invite them to send photos, email, or write letters describing their children as learners. There are still some teachers who arrange home visits, or invite students and parents to visit the classroom before school begins. Others launch classroom websites, student blogs, eportfolios, Fresh Grade entries and more while building an online community for classroom community – students, parents, and other invited guests. Whatever approach teachers choose, they can receive helpful information about students and their learning outside of school, as well as develop a better appreciation for the context of students' learning. Many parents appreciate the invitation to help the teacher understand what their son or daughter brings to the learning.

Goal setting conferences

Another way to build successful learning communities is to invite parents or guardians to participate in goal setting conferences early in the school year. During goal setting conferences, students and parents first meet at home and talk about the student's strengths and those areas needing improvement. They set learning goals together. The student and parents then meet with the teacher (in person, online, or on paper) and shares with the teacher information about the student as a learner. The teacher takes notes and asks questions. This process provides teachers with powerful information about students as learners, and allows students and parents to be heard.

Here's how one teacher describes the process and benefits of goal setting conferences in his elementary class.

> Every year we have a meeting with the parents about what the students are going to be learning. A few years ago we started having the parents bring

the children. Last year I decided that we were missing an opportunity to find out more about the kids as learners. I wanted the parent and child to think about what the child was good at and what she or he needed to work on, as well as what kinds of goals they wanted to achieve during the year. I gave each student a sheet to take home. It was sort of like a survey for the child and the parent. The students had to think about what they were really good at, what they were really proud of, what they wanted to get better at, and how they could help themselves learn. The parents were asked to write about the same things and to say how they could help their child. I asked them to bring along anything they wanted me to see.

It was amazing. When they came for their conferences, I got to listen to students talk about themselves as learners. The parents were so impressed. I listened to the parents talk about the child as a learner. The students just beamed. I asked questions and took notes. I found out so many things that I don't think I would ever have found out if I hadn't asked. It helped me when I was preparing for different units because I knew some of the kids knew more than I ever would. Also a couple of kids who weren't great at school had amazing talents – talents they were known for outside of school, such as being able to fix all kinds of small engines. Because I knew all about these incredible talents and expertise, I was able to help them gain equal status in our class.

For the conference, I gave people 20-minute time slots – we met at lunch, after school, and one evening. I also used the open-house night. It was worth every minute. Next year, our staff is talking about moving one of the conference days to early in the year so we can all do these kinds of conferences.

Research Connection:

Longitudinal studies identifying factors that lead to resilience in students from at-risk environments report that when students have conversations with parent substitutes, such as grandparents and older siblings, and have an external support system that rewards competence and provides them with a sense of coherence, they are more likely to be resilient. (Dweck 2000; NSCDC 2015; Werner and Smith 1992)

Checking in

Many months can go by while gathering enough reliable data to figure out what is going on with a particular child in order to provide the best learning opportunity, based solely on your own professional assessments. Checking in with students and parents benefits everyone.

After you complete your initial assessments at the beginning of the year, consider checking with students and parents if something doesn't make sense, or if students are significantly behind in their learning. Most schools and systems encourage teachers to seek help from school-based teams if students are more than two years behind.

When you are trying to make sense of the evidence you collect during the year, consider checking with students and parents. Take your assessment findings to the student and say, "This is what I see. Does it make sense to you?" Go to the parents and say, "This is what I see. What do you see? Am I on track here? Do you have anything to add?"

Research Connection:

When parents are involved in talking about learning with their children, children achieve more. The more parents are involved, the higher the student achievement levels. (Henderson and Berla 1994; NSCDC 2015)

A Community of Learners

Relationships are key. When we begin by sharing the learning destination with students and parents, and by building classroom agreements, we help build a community where learning is supported by assessment. Learning is only possible when everyone agrees that making mistakes, giving and receiving feedback, and taking time to self-assess and to learn are essential. Only when we work together can the foundation for classroom assessment – and learning – be established.

❝He who takes the wrong road must make his journey twice over.**❞**

Spanish Proverb

Guiding Our Own Learning

Think of a time when you learned something successfully. Make some notes about what you learned, when and where you learned it, who helped you, how they helped, and what kind of feedback you got. Talk with others about your experiences.

Build a common list of the kinds of feedback you found supportive for your learning. Consider and then talk about the implications for your students' learning and your teaching.

Take time to reflect. *How can you use this information to help your students learn more? How can you begin to give up responsibility for being the main source of feedback in the classroom? How can you create opportunities for students to get feedback for themselves that helps their learning?*

Guiding the Learning of Students

As a group, ask students to brainstorm their responses to the following question: *What counts in quality work?*

Then, as individuals, ask students to respond to the following question in writing: *What kind of feedback helps me do a better job?* Give examples and explain why.

Reflect on their responses, considering whether your students are well-served by their notions of quality and their understanding of feedback for learning.

You might want to spend some time sharing the research around feedback with them and talking about your expectations of what they need to know, be able to do and articulate in order to produce quality work.

Beginning with the End in Mind

" Students can reach any target that they know about and that holds still for them. " ✔

Rick Stiggins

When golfers swing their golf clubs, they know where to aim – toward the flag marking the next hole. Pilots file flight plans before getting permission to leave the ground. Successful gardeners plan for a new season, knowing what they want their garden to look like. Life coaches ask us to follow a similar process when they suggest we *begin with the end in mind*. It seems obvious that reaching a destination is easier if you know where or what it is. That's the point educational theorist Ralph Tyler (1949) was making many years ago, when he said that the first question a teacher needs to answer is: *What do I* ∞ *want my students to learn?* Yet, answering that question has been harder than we thought.

In North America, education standards or outcomes refer to that which students are expected to learn (that by which they will be judged). Standards and learning outcomes provide both opportunity as well as challenge. They are a guide for teaching and student learning. When teachers and students know where they are going, they are more likely to achieve success. When teachers know what needs to be learned and what students already know, they can plan a variety of learning pathways for students. Furthermore, students can provide a variety of evidence of having met the standard or achieved the learning outcome. Standards pose a challenge when quality expectations are unclear, when students arrive in class with differing levels of expertise, or if test results are all that matter. Challenges can become opportunities, with careful planning and thought.

Challenge: When quality expectations are unclear

If we have the written standard or outcome, but we don't understand the level of quality that is expected, then we won't know when our students have reached it. What is the opportunity here? Some jurisdictions are working to develop exemplars or samples to show what learning can look like over time. When we are able to access and use samples that show what the steps toward quality look like, the learning destination becomes clearer. Consider talking with your colleagues and looking at student work across grade levels.

Challenge: When students arrive in class with differing levels of expertise

Lists of standards or learning outcomes seem to assume that all students start in the same place, at the same time, and proceed to learn in the same way. This has never been true. Today, teachers find out what students already know, can do, and can articulate, and then they teach. The result is that teachers must learn more and more ways to teach to an ever-increasing range of student needs. One part of this challenge is having a comprehensive understanding of one's subject matter, in order to help students learn. The second challenge is learning how to teach small groups within the class rather than always teaching to the large group of students. Consider problem-solving with your colleagues - inviting their expertise in addressing challenging teaching dilemmas.

Challenge: When test results are all that matter

Sometimes standards are expressed in a way that seems to assume the learning will be shown in a certain form. Or, in some cases, the only measure of success is an external examination. This is a problem, since the more we limit the *form* evidence (or proof of learning) will take, the more some students will be unable to show what they know. When external assessments are balanced by high quality classroom level assessment, students have the time and experiences needed to learn, as well as a variety of ways to show what they know. Consider explaining to students and parents why tests are not enough and show current examples of other ways learning can be assessed and evaluated.

Researchers reporting from the field of neuroscience (Langer 1997; Pinker 1997; Pert 1999; and Restak 2003) say that when we know what we're going to be doing, we mentally prepare ourselves and activate more of our brain by doing so. Once students know what they are supposed to be learning, they can self-monitor, make adjustments, and learn more. From the teacher's point of view, there are three steps to this process:

1. Describe the learning destination so students and parents understand.
2. Share with students.
3. Use it.

The focus of this chapter is on how to develop a clear description of the learning destination.

Describing the Learning Destination

Teachers find that a description of what needs to be learned helps students learn more. While an educational system may define the learning in broad terms throughout its documents, teachers must translate and summarize the hundreds of statements into language that students and parents can understand.

Teachers develop descriptions by analyzing curriculum standards documents, grade-level expectations, descriptions of standards and expectations, and professional standards documents, such as NCTM Mathematics Standards. To this they add their personal reflections on their own professional experience. To the right is a sample description of 7th grade learning outcomes in Math.

> Profile of a 7th grade Math Student
> · has mastered basic operations
> · produces quality work
> · can communicate mathematical ideas effectively
> · is able to solve problems
> · can represent mathematical situations in multiple ways
> · gives logical arguments defending their answers
> · makes connections within and outside of mathematics
> · knows when to use appropriate tools in math
> · is able to design experiments & surveys to collect, organize, and analyze data

For most people, writing descriptions of learning goals is harder than it looks. Words easily obscure meaning, so start small. Choose one subject area or one unit of study for a focus. Summarize the outcomes or goals in simple, clear language that corresponds to how the learning needs to be reported later.

Read and review the curriculum expectations for your subject and grade level, checking back to the documents to see if there is anything you missed.

This example shows one group's first draft of describing the learning for Grade 7 French. The left column is not a list of the actual learning outcomes from the curriculum document, but instead the teachers' initial summary. Even at this early stage, these teachers found it useful to think ahead and consider possible sources of evidence.

French 7

Learning Outcomes	Possible Evidence
① willingly participates in all activities (esp. oral)	① checklist (observation)
② willingly takes risks	② volunteers consistently (instead of being asked)
③ positive attitude towards a 2nd language, culture	③ by observation
④ shows practice of vocabulary and structures	④ tests, quizzes, daily work
⑤ works cooperatively with partner +/or small groups	⑤ observation – product production – group evaluation
⑥ shows independence in learning ie /uses resources	⑥ looks in Fr/Eng dictionary before asking
⑦ can demonstrate learning visually, orally, and in writing	⑦ projects, assignments, presentations
⑧ makes connections outside of classroom + subject area	⑧ observations & projects

Sharing With Students

Sometimes classrooms are places where the only person who knows what needs to be learned is the teacher. This is a mistake. If students don't know what they are to learn and what it can look like, they are handicapped and their success is at risk. The time has passed when it is acceptable for students to turn up in classrooms and try to do their best without knowing what they need to learn. Students need their learning destination clearly stated – then it can be their flag, their flight plan, or simply a vision of success. It is true that not all students need this. Some students seem to know what you want them to learn before you do; others don't. This is typically a problem for those who struggle academically in our classrooms. They need teachers to be explicit about what needs to be learned. ∽

Using It

Teachers have many diverse ways of designing their descriptions to make them easy to use during the year, and to align them with school and district reporting requirements. Descriptions vary from place to place because the context differs, and each jurisdiction has its own unique way to use terms. Only you know how to communicate best to colleagues, students, and parents in your school community.

Few teachers begin with a blank slate – we make decisions based on the realities of our work and we all make different decisions based on our individual contexts. Here are some examples of ways teachers develop and use descriptions of learning:

Mrs. H has to prepare a narrative report card for her early primary class at the end of each term. As part of her assessment and evaluation process, she has reviewed all the documents related to reading and summarized them on an 11 by 17 inch sheet. She shows this sheet to students and explains what it is. She also posts it for parents to see. This summary of what needs to be learned assists her in tracking her students' learning. Later, it is a valuable resource for the student-parent-teacher conference held at the end of the term and for the narrative report card she prepares for each student.

Mr. R teaches Grade 4. He has to report using a report card that includes a developmental continuum. He makes a copy of the report card and uses the developmental continuum as a summary guide of the elements that he needs to teach and assess. He shares this with students and parents so they all know what he is assessing. ✓

Mr. M uses a three-way reporting process in his Grade 6 class. In this process, students do self-reports, the teacher does a report, and the parents review the evidence and are also invited to report. In order that students (and parents) are prepared to be a part of the reporting process, Mr. M has a description of what students will be learning in each mathematics strand. He posts the description at the beginning of each unit. Students also collect evidence related to each part of the description so they will be ready to show their parents the evidence during their conference. When Mr. M's class received laptops for every student, the same process continued to work, with students collecting and presenting their information and accompanying reflections in digital form.

<table>
<tr><th colspan="2" align="center">GRADE 9 ENGLISH</th></tr>
<tr>
<td>

DESTINATION

Students will, in a consistent, self-directed and independent manner...

- Produce quality pieces of writing
- Demonstrate understanding of the elements of narrative
- Develop English language skills
- Effectively communicate ideas and share products with others
- Effectively collaborate with peers in the learning process
- Collect evidence of learning in a portfolio
- Assess the work of self and others in a thoughtful and productive manner

</td>
<td>

EVIDENCE

- writing pieces: autobiographical short stories
- reading responses
- plot diagrams
- video/audio tape of oral storytelling
- illustrations
- journal entries
- self and peer assessments
- large/small group participation
- working independently
- presenting work to others

</td>
</tr>
<tr>
<td>

SAMPLES/MODELS

- past student writing samples
- sample videotape of past student oral presentations
- past student samples of vocabulary notebooks
- in-class modeling of plot diagrams
- samples of past student reading responses
- samples of past student journals

</td>
<td>

EVALUATION

- produces quality written assignments that:
  - meet set criteria
  - show multiple drafts that are edited and revised for content, spelling, grammar and punctuation (product)
- produces reading assignments that:
  - meet set criteria
  - show evidence of understanding the reading (product)
- consistently reflects upon work and learning in a thoughtful and directed manner (conversation)
- works cooperatively and independently in producing and presenting work (observation)

</td>
</tr>
</table>

Ms. G teaches Grade 9 English. Although she agrees with research showing that letter grades may get in the way of learning (see page 18 of this book), she is still required to give letter grades, and so she does. She tries to "compensate for the compulsory" by being clear with students about what is expected and what success looks like. She drafts a description of what success looks like in Grade 9 English. This description is a series of statements describing what students are to know and be able to do.

Mr. D teaches a university-level course. He wants students to value the learning so he shows them how he will evaluate it. He provides a detailed description of what students need to know, do and articulate, along with a list of possible evidence of learning. Students are told to collect all possible evidence as the course proceeds so they can submit what is needed to show proof of learning and quality.

The Development Cycle

Teachers develop descriptions that take into account what needs to be learned and how the learning needs to be reported. Developing and using descriptions is part of the assessment-learning cycle. When we explain to students what they need to learn and we answer their questions, they gain a better understanding of what counts. When the descriptions of what needs to be learned are accompanied by samples that show what success looks like, students begin to be informed enough to make choices that help their learning. Then, when students know what the evidence can look like, they become more able to show us what they know. As we use descriptions in classrooms, we find ways to express them more clearly – an ongoing process with each new group of students and parents. Consider the Mathematics example on this page. It details both the learning destination and the possible evidence of learning to be collected.

Mathematics – Defining an A	
Student consistently and independently ...	**Evidence of learning collected over time from multiple sources includes...**
• Understands, remembers and applies mathematical concepts being studied • Articulates clear understanding of mathematical concepts and is able to give everyday examples of use • Applies concepts, skills and strategies to problems • Analyzes problems, uses a variety of effective strategies to find possible solutions, and is able to check and evaluate the effectiveness of the process used • Works effectively by self and with others • Communicates effectively using words, symbols, and representations • Connects ideas to self, to others and to other ideas or tasks • Uses mathematical 'habits of mind' including, for example, persistence, questioning, drawing on past knowledge, precision of language and thought	Ongoing work samples, such as: • Products (e.g. work samples, tests, quizzes) • Observations (e.g. class work, demonstrations performance tasks, teacher observations) • Conversations (e.g. discussions, written reflections, journal entries, conferences, interviews) **Evaluations include:** • Common assessment scores: (Typically 4's) • Evaluations, such as performance tasks, projects, tests and quizzes, receive grades in the 91% – 100% range.

❝*If you don't know where you are going, every road will get you nowhere.***❞**

Henry Kissinger

Guiding Our Own Learning

Begin to draft your own assessment plan by considering the following steps:

1. Choose a subject area and one term to focus on. You may find it easier to begin with one unit of study.
2. Summarize the learning goals (also called learning standards or learning outcomes) into a clear description of the learning destination.
3. Read and review the documents for your subject area and grade level to see if your description is an accurate summary.
4. Check your description with a colleague, as well as someone you know who does not work in education. Ask for feedback that focuses on ways to make it clear and simple enough so that others can easily understand the learning destination.

Guiding the Learning of Students

Ask your students to read your draft of one learning destination and tell you what it means. Talk about it. Ask them for suggestions for any changes that will make it more easily understood by them and their parents.

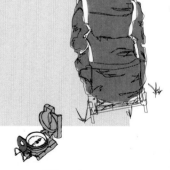

Chapter 4

Describing Success

❝ Students can assess themselves only when they have a sufficiently clear picture of the targets their learning is meant to attain. ❞

Black and Wiliam

"What do you want?" says a student. "How good is good enough?" asks a colleague. "What does excellence look like?" you wonder. These are questions that relate to standards or learning outcomes. Educational guidelines provide a list of learning expectations for each grade level. However, standards often define what students need to learn and be able to do without *showing* what it looks like when they do. For example, "communicates effectively in writing" looks different for a seven-year-old than for a sixteen-year-old. Teachers may know what the standard says but have no idea what it looks like for students of a particular age. Furthermore, if teachers are not clear what reaching success looks like for their students, they will not know when their students have reached it.

As mentioned earlier, standards seem to assume that all students start in the same place, at the same time, and proceed to learn in the same way. Teachers know that learning is not sequential. Students learn in different ways and at different rates; there will never be a class where all the students are the same. Thus, if teachers provide only a few options for students to demonstrate their learning, they can limit students' ability or opportunity to show what they know. Samples can help. Excellence can be revealed in a multitude of ways. As the diversity increases among our students, whether from learning styles, culture and language, family circumstances, or countless other factors, teachers need to learn how to allow for differences and to work toward students meeting standards. Then, diversity can be a source of strength in our communities and in our classrooms. Evidence of learning needs to be diverse because it requires performance and self-assessment or reflection to demonstrate application and the ability to articulate understandings. This means that written work or test results can never be enough. Observing application of knowledge, listening to students articulate understandings, and engaging students in demonstrating acquisition of knowledge can be valid evidence. Collections of samples, models, and criteria help students and others appreciate the need for a range of evidence of learning.

Sample and Exemplar Collections

Samples and exemplar collections can take many forms, including maps, reading responses, writing projects, mathematical thinking, problem-solving, videos of oral presentations, computer animations or research projects – anything that illustrates what students are expected to know and do in the classroom. Effective samples of student work illustrate the description of learning and answer the question: *What will it look like when I've learned it?* Using samples to represent the levels of quality involved in meeting standards can serve not only to help students understand the expectations, but also to improve the professional judgments of teachers.

Using Samples in Classrooms: What does it look like?

Samples are important if quality classroom assessment is going to be effective. Samples, exemplars, models, or demonstrations can support teachers to:

- develop criteria with students
- assess and give descriptive feedback about student work
- show ways to represent their learning (give evidence)
- help others understand more about student learning
- inform professional judgment

Using samples to develop criteria with students

Collections of student samples illustrate for teachers what students can do, and help students develop a sense of what is important. When students analyze samples, they begin to understand what student work looks like at different points on its way to the standard. They also begin to internalize the criteria that will be used to assess their work. When students understand what is important, they have an opportunity to assess their own efforts in regard to the criteria, and give themselves specific, descriptive feedback about their own learning as they progress.

Setting and Using Criteria, 2nd Edition (Gregory, Cameron, and Davies 2011a) outlines a process for developing criteria with students:

1. Make a brainstormed list.
2. Sort and categorize the list.
3. Make and post a T-chart.
4. Use and revisit and revise.

When using samples to develop criteria in relation to evidence of learning (both products and processes), students first examine the samples and list the important features. The teacher records student ideas as a brainstormed list and may also add to the list. Once the list is complete, the ideas are sorted and put into a T-chart that can be posted in the class. The list of criteria is then used to help students self-assess, to give descriptive feedback and to assess student work.

Using samples to assess student work and give feedback

If the criteria are clear and samples available, then there are many options for responding to student work and giving descriptive feedback. For example, students can compare their work to samples in order to see what is working or what needs attention. Samples might be used to show the range of acceptable work, to show what outstanding work looks like, or to show the many different ways students can demonstrate what they have learned. Teachers need to decide when it is appropriate to use samples in order to support student learning, since they could be a hindrance if used at the wrong time or in the wrong way. Here are some examples of ways in which teachers are using samples to support learning.

> Ms. S asks students to practice their reading in partners. While one partner is reading, the other is observing those things that show he or she is a good reader. The observer has a record sheet, created by the students, that lists characteristics of good reading. Each partner gives the other specific, descriptive feedback using the criteria on the record sheets.

Mr. M posts samples and criteria on his school's website so students and parents can access them easily. Students (and others) use the samples and the criteria to give themselves and their peers specific, descriptive feedback.

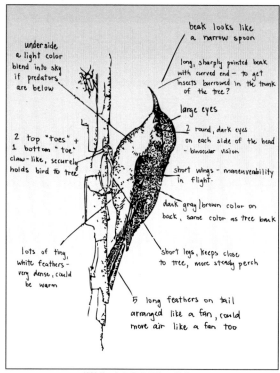

With thanks to Polly Wilson, Maine

Ms. L has a collection of line drawings, paintings, prints, and sculpture to show art development over time. She asks students to analyze different pieces prior to self-assessing or giving peer feedback. This practice helps them become more specific in their feedback to themselves and others, and is therefore, more helpful for further learning.

Mr. R has a collection of research projects from previous years to show his students what is possible and what success might look like. Prior to beginning a research project, he asks students to work in groups to analyze the projects. Then, as a whole class, they develop criteria to guide their work towards quality.

Ms. Z posts two or three numbered samples of maps with the criteria that the class developed with her assistance. Prior to meeting for peer feedback, students are given time to compare their work to the samples. They record which sample their work most resembles and why.

Mr. C posts two samples of reader responses to show students the way to quality. While their work is in progress, students are asked to compare their responses to the samples. Later, students may be asked to self-assess in relation to the criteria posted with the samples, or to decide which sample their work most resembles and why. This self-assessment is attached to their work and submitted to the teacher.

Ms. D and Mr. L both ask their high school students to donate a copy of their portfolios - digital or print - for them to use with subsequent classes. Each year a few students are happy to do so. The teachers use these portfolios to demonstrate to their Social Studies and Mathematics students how their portfolios might look. They also lead a discussion about what could make the portfolio more effective.

Using samples to show ways to represent learning

Teachers will often use samples to help students see the range of development over time – for example, a series of writing samples that show development towards increasing quality. Teachers will also use samples to illustrate the many ways students can represent what they've learned. When students are able to select different ways to show what they've learned, more students are likely to be able to show their learning and the form of representation is less likely to be a barrier to their success.

With thanks to Pauoa School, Hawaii

Using samples to help others understand learning

Showing samples can help teachers answer students' questions – "What do you want?" "How good is good enough?" "What does excellence look like?" – by illustrating the standard. Comparing student work to samples, models and criteria can also help us respond to the parent who asks, "How is my child doing?" or to others who ask to see proof of student learning. When meeting with parents, teachers use collections of samples to show the gap between the student's current level of quality and the next level. This helps parents understand the ways they might support future learning. When others look at children's collections of evidence of learning and compare them to the quality expected by the standards, they gain insights that help close the achievement gap.

Using samples to inform professional judgment

Collections that illustrate standards can be developed by working with colleagues to gather and analyze samples that illustrate quality. Teachers collect different samples depending on the standards towards which they teach, their grade level, and their students' needs. Examining student work in comparison to criteria has been shown to improve teachers' professional judgment (Adie and Willis 2016; ARG 2006; Wyatt-Smith and Klenoski 2008).

Here are some more ways teachers have used samples to support classroom assessment:

Ms. M used samples of student writing (drawings, letters, groups of letters, words) to help her kindergarten students understand writing development. The first sample was one every child in the class could produce easily. The second sample was a little further along the continuum. Every few days, Ms. M brought in another sample. When she introduced each one, she asked the students what the sample showed about quality writing. Together they made a verbal list. Then she asked what the writer could have done to improve each writing sample. Students used this work to guide their learning as well as their self-assessment. Ms. M used it to point out ideas to students and demonstrate ways they could improve their own writing.

Ms. J decided that one way to illustrate standards for reading in Grade 2 was to put together a collection of book titles and authors to show the range of what students at this level read. She based her collection on her own experience and suggestions from colleagues. She posted the list on the school website so parents could refer to it from time to time, as their child progressed.

Mr. V gathered work from his Grade 4 students and from colleagues to make files of six to ten samples, showing the range of writing that children of this age can produce, in each of the following three general categories:
- personal experience
- narratives
- communicating information

Mr. T worked with his students to put together a large collection of products which they digitized to make both sharing and storage easier. The items collected demonstrated a range of mathematical thinking and problem-solving at the Grade 7 level. These included:

- journal entries that show problem-solving
- notebooks (including some from previous years)
- "before" and "after" portfolio entries
- sample questions that students designed for partners to solve

Over the past three years, Ms. B has built a collection of digital samples that shows the range of reading and writing that students in Grade 11 can do. These include:

- reader response journal entries
- lists of books read by students
- sample paragraphs
- projects (posters, literary maps, character analyses, and oral presentations captured on video)

Ms. D teaches a fifth-year university history course. She collects a range of samples of assignments from some students each term, as well as some of the final exam questions and answers. Each assignment has an attached performance rubric (developed with students). Although there are no column labels, letter grades or scaled numbers as headings, it is clear from the description that the level of quality changes from column to column. The discussion with students gives them a sense of the different ways that quality work can look at this level. She is careful to ensure that the specific details provide descriptive (not evaluative) feedback. For example, the description might say "needs to be edited for spelling" (descriptive feedback) rather than "lots of spelling errors" (evaluative feedback). Students are able to resubmit assignments up until a few days before she begins preparing to assign final grades.

Mr. R is a learning resource teacher in an elementary school setting. He has a collection of student writing samples showing stages of development, from drawings with letter-like forms to student-written chapter books. He has put them into an accordion-style construction paper booklet that can be kept on a bookshelf but unfolds to create a long display, like a frieze. When he is working with students, he displays the one most like the student's work and another at the next quality level. Then, together, they plan the next steps for improvement.

Collecting and Analyzing Samples

Teachers can collect samples by themselves over time, but it is easier and more powerful if done with colleagues. The process of analyzing and selecting samples gives teachers the chance to see a broad range of student work, understand what students are to know, develop a commonly held sense of what the learning might look like for students over time, and begin to develop a common language to use. Here is one process you could follow:

1. Find some interested and willing colleagues.
2. Choose a focus for your investigation (e.g., journal writing).
3. Collect a range of samples. (Ensure that they are anonymous.)
4. Analyze what is working and what the next teaching steps could be for each sample. (Compare your student samples to exemplars provided by provincial or state assessments, if available.)
5. Build a personal collection.
6. Choose another focus and repeat the cycle.

Ways to Come to Common Agreement about Quality

Purpose: To engage all participants and resource people in discussing and determining quality level work.

Prior to the Conversation: The professional learning team identifies an area of quality work upon which to focus. Each participant brings two or three samples of student work, of which at least one is determined to be 'at grade level.' All student names are removed or covered and work is labeled with a number such as 1, 2, or 3. Copies of the work are made for everyone. If student work is lengthy, the work and the focus question may be given ahead of time. The presenting educator identifies a focus question for the feedback – Would you agree this is 'at grade level' work? The presenting educator completes a written assessment before beginning the critique (see Preparatory Self-Assessment below) and prepares a five-minute overview of the work.

Time needed: 30 – 35 minutes for each review.

1. **Getting Started:** Select a facilitator and a timekeeper. Review the purpose of the protocol and ground rules for this process.
2. **Describing the Context:** The presenting teacher offers any background information and the purpose for the assessment. The focus question is written on chart paper or the board for all to see.
3. **Seeking Understanding:** Three reviewers ask questions to clarify. (3 minutes)
4. **Reviewing the Work:** Group members review the work. They discuss where the work is of quality in terms of the criteria used by students, what could improve the work and possible next learning and teaching steps for each student. (8 minutes)
5. **Extending the Connections:** The presenting teacher joins the conversation and directs it to any intriguing ideas or points to pursue. (3 minutes)
6. **Summarizing the Ideas:** Each participant has a last word to sum up the conversation. (5 minutes)
7. **Reflecting on the Conversation:** Presenter(s) of the work and Reviewers comment briefly on the effectiveness of the protocol. (3 minutes)
8. **Continuing the Learning:** Repeat for each work presented.

Preparatory Self-Assessment:
- The learning purpose that students were given for this work was:
- The learning context for this work was:
- The criteria for success for this work was:
- I assess these samples as being of grade-level quality because...
- In order to improve the quality of these samples, students would need to show evidence or be able to do...
- I think the next learning steps for these students are...

Adapted with permission from *Protocols for Professional Learning Conversations* by Catherine Glaude
Published by Connections Publishing (2005)

Here are some descriptions of how others have worked to gather samples. In some cases, the samples from provincial and state assessments were used to clarify understanding of standards; in others, they were used to actually establish standards for educational jurisdictions. In all cases, students' names and grade levels were removed from the samples.

A teacher leads

Mr. M was new to Middle School (grades 6 to 8) and unsure of the kind of Readers' Theatre that students of this age were capable of performing. He put out a request asking teachers to share any samples of scripts, videos of performances they might have collected over the years, as well as examples of students' RT performances online. He also offered to copy and collate the collection, as well as add his students' work to the collection later. Three teachers responded, permissions were obtained, and a collection of samples and video presentations was made and distributed.

Readers' Theatre	
Criteria	Details
Performers' positions help communicate the message.	- some readers were elevated - audience can see everyone they are supposed to see - scripts don't make noise
Performers' voices communicate meaning.	- words are clear (enunciation) - readers' voices change to match script and characters - readers can read the script - there aren't any big silences
Performers' actions help audience listen and understand	- rehearsed - props help audience understand - performers enter and exit smoothly - everyone bows together - people turn when they are supposed to

Adapted from Dixon, Davies and Politano, *Learning with Readers Theatre*, 71

Whole-school participation

One school wanted to learn more about what good writing looked like for students of different ages. The teaching faculty all agreed to collect first-draft journal-writing samples that showed the range of writing in their classes and to bring at least six samples that showed a range of student learning and achievement to the next meeting.

Copies were made of the samples so everyone could look at them. Sitting in grade-level groups, the teachers looked at all the samples, talked about what was typical for this age range, what was outstanding, and what would be of concern. They selected some from the entire group of samples that showed the range of what students were able to do at their grade level. They also used a protocol to guide this conversation (e.g., Glaude, 2005).

After members of grade-level groups had analyzed and selected samples, they listed what the students were capable of as writers at each level. Recorders took notes. They also brainstormed one or two possible "next steps" in terms of instruction, based on the needs evident in each sample.

Near the end of the three-hour period, the teachers reviewed the work samples of students from the youngest to the oldest in the school, in order to have a sense of development over time. The writing samples were collected and placed in a binder for teachers and parents. Later, when the education department published a collection of writing samples, the group reviewed them and added additional samples to their collection.

The next topic this staff chose to learn more about was reading development. They did this by collecting reader responses from a wide range of students. They also involved staff from a neighbouring school, which increased the breadth of expertise of the reviewers and the range of student samples. Both schools got a copy of the samples, the analysis and the next teaching steps.

After analyzing large numbers of writing samples, a group developed a description of writing development from K to 12. In order to help teachers understand the description, the group collected samples to illustrate what students know and are able to do at different grade levels – development over time, from kindergarten to graduation – and the *range* of development that could be expected at different ages.

More and more, jurisdictions are collecting a vast range of exemplars for different subject areas. Some of these can be found easily available online. These samples can be used in a variety of ways by classroom teachers to:

- develop criteria for different kinds of evidence of learning with students
- provide better quality feedback
- help others understand learning
- increase the accuracy of one's professional judgment

When using samples and exemplars, it is important to continue to acknowledge that students learn in different ways and at different rates. Teachers are making sense of standards by starting with students and their work, and talking with colleagues. Don't forget to also involve students. Consider challenging them to find samples and exemplars to help illustrate quality development over time. Our job is to be thoughtful and as curious as possible about how our students learn and how to use assessment to support their learning.

" We advance on our journey only when we face our goal, when we are confident and believe we are going to win out. "

Orison Swett Marden

Guiding Our Own Learning

With colleagues or on your own, choose one area of focus and collect a range of samples. Remove all identifying features. It is important that students not be able to identify another student's work. You may need to trade samples with a colleague from another school. Or, ask students to create samples just for this purpose.

As you review the samples, make a list of what you see in each sample that is important for students to notice. Later, as students analyze samples, they will often add other important features and ideas to the list.

Guiding the Learning of Students

Ask students to look at the collected samples. You might choose to look at only one or two in the beginning. Record what they think is important. Draw their attention to any features they are missing. Then, ask for suggestions of one or two things that could have been done to improve the quality of the sample. Suggest they use the sample to guide their own work towards quality.

Evidence of Learning

"Only if we expand and reformulate our view of what counts as human intellect will we be able to devise more appropriate ways of assessing it and more effective ways of educating it."
Howard Gardner

Contents

Once you have described what students need to learn and have developed a sense of what success might look like for your students, it is time to consider what kinds of evidence you will need to collect, in order to plan ongoing instruction and ensure validity and reliability of your professional judgment and your summative evaluation. That way, when you evaluate at the end of the learning period, you and others can have confidence that you will be able to make high quality professional judgments and base your teaching on evidence of student learning needs.

Different teachers collect different kinds of evidence, even though the description of what their students need to learn may be the same. This is because the learning experiences that teachers design for different groups of learners may vary. Also, since students learn in different ways and at different times, collections of evidence may vary slightly in terms of how students choose to represent their learning. When making lists of the evidence to collect, teachers need to make sure they plan to gather evidence from a variety of sources, and that they gather evidence over time.

Sources of Evidence

There are three general sources of assessment evidence gathered in classrooms: *observations* of learning, *products* students create, and *conversations* with students about learning (Primary Program 2000).

When evidence is collected from three different sources over time, trends and patterns become apparent, and the reliability and validity of our classroom assessment is increased. This process is called *triangulation* (Lincoln and Guba 1984).

Reliability: think "repeatability" – reliability refers to students producing the same kind of result at different times.

Validity: think "valid" – the extent to which the evidence from multiple sources matches the quality levels expected in light of the standards or learning outcomes.

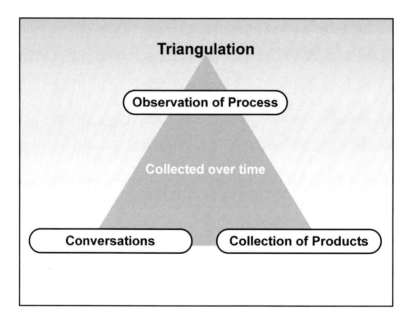

Observing the Learning

The list of evidence you plan to collect needs to include the observations you will make while students are learning. The record of observations becomes evidence.

You might observe . . . formal and informal presentations, drama presentations, scientific method being applied, music-related activities, reading aloud, group or partner activities, talking about one's own work, planning and designing a Web page, persuading, giving opinions, following instructions, listening to others, arguing, predicting, measuring objects, charades, dances, communicating ideas to others in a small group setting, conflict resolution, discussions, giving and receiving descriptive feedback, working with partners or in teams, identifying sounds, rhythm games, cartooning, playing instruments, jigsaws, demonstrations, any skills development, movement exercises, keyboarding, gestures, pantomimes, re-enactments, gymnastic routines, sign language, graphic design, simulations, debating, answering questions, presenting own work, giving instructions, singing, telling stories, verbalizing abstract reasoning, sculpture, choral readings, conversations, dialogues, dramatic readings, oral descriptions, oral reports, plays, puppet shows, Readers' Theatre, storytelling, demonstrating symbolic thinking, teaching a lesson, creating a slide show, role plays, verbal explanations, and verbal instructions. This list could include anything a teacher might observe students doing or might ask them to do. Thanks to technology students can also collect observations of themselves or their peers.

Observations are essential if your classroom assessment and evaluation are to be reliable and valid. In addition to being necessary for triangulating your evidence, some learning can only be observed. For example, some students are better able to show what they know by doing it. These "in action" kinds of learners and younger children, who are able to record little in writing, need some of their learning assessed through observation. Also, products "under construction" can provide teachers with opportunities to observe students' learning. Without enough observational evidence, our evaluations at report card time risk being invalid.

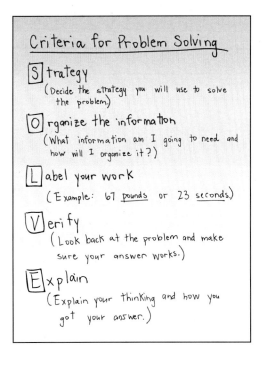

Criteria for Problem Solving

Strategy
(Decide the strategy you will use to solve the problem.)

Organize the information
(What information am I going to need and how will I organize it?)

Label your work
(Example: 67 pounds or 23 seconds.)

Verify
(Look back at the problem and make sure your answer works.)

Explain
(Explain your thinking and how you got your answer.)

Teachers have different ways of recording their observations. The key is that observations need to be focused to ensure that the information you are recording is related to the description of what students are to learn. It is usually not enough to observe that a student completed his math work. Rather, you would observe what skill was practiced, what level of skill the student was observed as demonstrating, and perhaps some possible next steps for instruction. For example, if students are practicing two-digit addition, you might choose to observe and record the level of difficulty of the questions that the students choose to practice: e.g., addition without regrouping, addition with regrouping. These observations may be used to form your teaching groups the next day, or to determine the subject of your math mini-lesson and the next day's practice activities. The same observations will later form part of the evidence that you will examine when you evaluate the students' progress in mathematics.

Spelling Focus
- journal writing
- observing prefixes and suffixes

✓ observed
— not observed
O needs help

Date
Oct. 14
Nov. 10

Anna ✓ dis, un / ✓	Bob ✓ un, ing / ✓	Concordia es, dis / ✓	Carl dis, re / ✓	Chin — / ✓ dis, re, es, ed	Don ✓ es / ✓	Elaine — / ✓ ing, ed, es	Elvin — / ✓ ing, dis, es
Kara — / ✓ un, dis	Kevin ✓ ing, un / ✓	Luis — / ✓	Nona — / ✓	Matt J. ✓ ed / ✓ es, re	Matt M. O ed, es consonant doubling / ✓ ed, ing, es? needs work	Parma O ed, es, c.d.? / ✓ ed, es, dis, on	Robert ✓ ex, un / ✓ dis, ed
Ryland ✓ dis / ✓ ed, ing	Stefan ✓ ing, re / ✓ dis, es, ed	Sidura ✓ ed, dis, ing / ✓ es, ed	Thang ✓ un, ing / ✓ es, ed	Val — / ✓ re, es, dis, ed	Zoe ✓ ing, es, ed, un / ✓ re, dis		

From Smith and Davies, *Wordsmithing*, 85

Math Problem Solving

Teacher _____ Grade _____

NAMES	/	/	/	/	/	/	/
RAHIM	SOLVE	SOLVE	SOLVE	SOLVE	SOLVE	SOLVE	SOLVE
OSA	SOLVE	SOLVE	SOLVE	SOLVE	SOLVE	SOLVE	SOLVE
ALEXI	SOLVE	SOLVE	SOLVE	SOLVE	SOLVE	SOLVE	SOLVE
ISAAC	SOLVE	SOLVE	SOLVE	SOLVE	SOLVE	SOLVE	SOLVE
JADE	SOLVE	SOLVE	SOLVE	SOLVE	SOLVE	SOLVE	SOLVE
TANIKA	SOLVE	SOLVE	SOLVE	SOLVE	SOLVE	SOLVE	SOLVE
KAYLA	SOLVE	SOLVE	SOLVE	SOLVE	SOLVE	SOLVE	SOLVE
HOLLY	SOLVE	SOLVE	SOLVE	SOLVE	SOLVE	SOLVE	SOLVE
DAKOTA	SOLVE	SOLVE	SOLVE	SOLVE	SOLVE	SOLVE	SOLVE

The focus of your observations depends on the purpose of the activity. If you can answer the following questions, then you are on your way to designing focused observations that will be useful in planning subsequent learning activities and will form a part of your evaluation later in the term.

- *What is the purpose of the learning activity? What are students to learn?*
- *What particular focus will I choose for this observation?*
- *How will I record and organize my observations so they are useful?*

Teachers analyze patterns and trends and, if needed, report observations collected over time in numeric form.

Collecting Products

Teachers collect various kinds of evidence to show what students can do. Classroom assessment is a process of evidentiary learning (Mislevy and Riconscente 2005). These include projects, assignments, notebooks, and tests. As advances in technology take place, we are rethinking old ideas about intelligence and evidence of learning. For example, early childhood teachers use photographs to document observations or activities e.g., photos of geometric structures built by students. When students are asked to represent what they know only in writing, some will be unable, due to their lack of skill as writers. However, when asked to demonstrate the process in action or to give an oral presentation, their knowledge and skill may rapidly become apparent.

More and more teachers are introducing an element of choice into the form that products may take. Some teachers create a list of ideas with their students. Over time, the list grows as students learn more about different ways of representing.

Conversations About Learning

We listen to learners during class meetings, at individual or group conferences, or when we read students' self-assessments about their work. We also have opportunities to listen when students assess their work in relation to criteria, analyze their work samples for their portfolios, or prepare to report to parents about their learning.

Different ways to show what we know...

- draw a diagram
- make a time line
- make a poster
- write a story
- do an oral presentation
- write a poem
- build a model
- design a Web page
- create a puzzle
- make a video
- create an iMovie
- make a podcast
- make a recording
- design a T-shirt
- do a report
- write a song
- create a collage
- build a diorama
- write a play
- do a journal entry
- perform a puppet show
- input e-journal entry

When we listen to students in these ways, we are inviting them to think about their learning. As they think and explain, we can gather evidence about what they know and understand. We can find out about what they did or created – such as, their best efforts, what was difficult or easy, what they might do differently next time, and what risks they take as learners. Students learn more when we take the time to involve them in self-assessment (Andrade 2011; Black and Wiliam 1998; Boud 2003; Johnston 2004). The ability to articulate their learning processes – as part of a readers response, a mathematics response or in some other way – has become an increasingly important aspect of classroom and external assessment.

Conversations about learning involve listening to what students have to say about their learning, or reading what they record about their learning. The "conversation" may be face-to-face, or recorded online in writing, audio, or video.

" *I can't say enough about how impressed I am by how specific and articulate my students have become as a result of setting criteria, doing reflections and keeping learning goals portfolios.* **"**

Holly Tornrose,
High School English Teacher

Creating a Plan

It takes some planning to make sure you have enough evidence, the right kind of evidence, and evidence that is reliable and valid. As teachers, we ensure reliability and validity by having proof of learning from multiple sources collected over time. We also plan to collect a range of evidence – both qualitative and quantitative data. We check the evidence we plan to collect by matching it to the curriculum standards for which we are responsible. We look at the learning destination and match it to the evidence asking: *Are there any gaps? Are there any overlaps? Am I collecting evidence from multiple sources and over time?*

How much evidence is enough?

There is no one right answer to this question. The amount of ongoing evidence needed to effectively plan daily instruction varies from teacher to teacher, depending on the subject, the teacher, the students, and the community in which they learn. Each teacher needs to determine the amount of evidence that works in his or her situation, given what students are learning.

One guideline to keep in mind is that you must have enough evidence to be able to identify patterns and trends in student learning. To do this, you need student work (evidence of learning) that accounts for the full range of what needs to be learned. The evidence needs to show learning over time.

Taking care...

Be aware of the important difference between *large-scale assessment* and *classroom assessment*. The purpose of *large-scale assessments* is two-fold: to help the system be accountable *(Are we making the best use of our resources?)* and to identify trends *(Are students learning? What are they learning? How well?)*. To do this, large-scale assessments need only to collect a small amount of information from a large number of students. These assessments are designed to determine what students know, can do and can articulate in relation to what is to be learned. They do not collect enough information to give a valid and complete picture of everything students know and are able to do at any point in time, in relation to all the standards or learning outcomes they are to learn. Large-scale assessments can only provide a *snapshot* of *some* of the learning. They are better designed to describe what groups of students are able to do.

Classroom assessment is quite different. Teachers and students collect a large amount of evidence over time from multiple sources. It is designed to account for all that is to be learned by individuals – student by student. When done well, classroom assessment is better able to give a more valid and reliable accounting of a student's learning.

How do I know I have the right kinds of evidence?

Evidence of learning may include observations, products, and conversations. The kind of assessment evidence collected from students needs to be appropriate to the type of learning. For example, paper-and-pencil tasks are a great way to assess knowledge of basic facts, but would be unsuitable for assessing oral presentation skills. Sorting out what kinds of evidence you need to show different kinds of learning is a necessary step in planning what to collect. If your evidence is triangulated, then you are likely using a range of techniques to gather proof of learning over time. This is key to having the right kind and balance of evidence. Only you can determine whether or not it satisfactorily addresses the range of what needs to be learned. Your professional judgment will improve as you develop clear achievement criteria for reporting purposes (for example, see page 31).

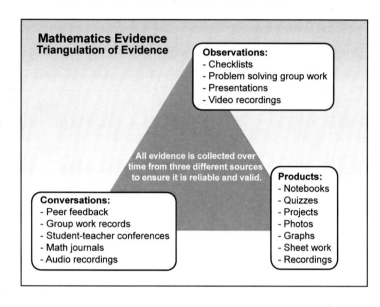

Mathematics Evidence
Triangulation of Evidence

Observations:
- Checklists
- Problem solving group work
- Presentations
- Video recordings

All evidence is collected over time from three different sources to ensure it is reliable and valid.

Conversations:
- Peer feedback
- Group work records
- Student-teacher conferences
- Math journals
- Audio recordings

Products:
- Notebooks
- Quizzes
- Projects
- Photos
- Graphs
- Sheet work
- Recordings

How can I be sure my evidence will help my evaluations be reliable and valid?

If you have collected enough evidence and the right kind of evidence, and have thoughtfully worked with colleagues to improve your professional judgment, then you can feel confident that your evaluations will be reliable and valid. In general, confidence increases when there is a wide range of evidence, when it is collected over time and when there are clear criteria that define quality. Remember that everything students do, say, and create is potential evidence. Consider assessing more and evaluating less. We interrupt learning if we evaluate too often, whereas assessment information can guide instruction and support learning.

When you get ready to evaluate and report on how well students are doing in relation to what needs to be learned, you will first need to review the description of learning, check that you have the right kinds of evidence, and use these *observations, products,* and *conversations* to answer the questions: *Did this student learn what she or he needed to learn? How well?* In order to make an evaluation, we may look at different collections of evidence for different students.

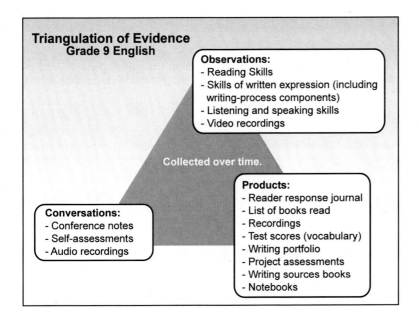

Triangulation of Evidence
Grade 9 English

Observations:
- Reading Skills
- Skills of written expression (including writing-process components)
- Listening and speaking skills
- Video recordings

Collected over time.

Products:
- Reader response journal
- List of books read
- Recordings
- Test scores (vocabulary)
- Writing portfolio
- Project assessments
- Writing sources books
- Notebooks

Conversations:
- Conference notes
- Self-assessments
- Audio recordings

It is important that we use the evidence available for each student and compare it to the same set of curriculum standards and expectations. In a standards-based evaluation system, we have to account for each student's learning in relation to the expectations for that grade and subject area. While our written and verbal comments may speak to the amount of progress students have made in their learning, the evaluation must reflect their accomplishments in relation to the standards for the subject area and level at which they are working.

“Even with the best of maps and instruments, we can never fully chart our journeys. ”

Gail Pool

Guiding Our Own Learning

Develop a plan for collecting evidence by returning to your earlier description of what students need to learn, be able to do, and be able to articulate (see *Guiding Our Own Learning* on page 32).

Think about the evidence of learning you and your students will be able to collect. Consider observations, products, and conversations. Make a list of all the evidence related to the learning destination.

When you are finished, review the list, asking yourself:
- Will my evidence show whether or not students have learned what they needed to learn?
- Is there any evidence I am collecting for which I am not accountable?
- Am I collecting evidence from multiple sources?
- Am I collecting enough evidence to see patterns over time?
- Am I collecting too much evidence? Is there anything I can stop collecting?
- How can my students be involved in collecting and organizing the evidence?

Show your draft to a trusted colleague. Ask if he or she thinks there is anything you have missed or anything you could delete. Consider the suggestions and make your own decision.

When we divide up the responsibility for developing the first draft, everyone benefits – we improve our work and have more confidence in it. Talk about your list of evidence with others. Share your list. Invite others to share their work with you. After you have piloted the process with one subject area, proceed to do the same with other subject areas or courses.

Guiding the Learning of Students

Prepare the students to *assess their way to success* by asking them to identify all the evidence they might have that shows proof of meeting the learning destination. Ask them to consider not only what *you* would need for proof but also what *others* (i.e. parents, employers, other institutions) would need for proof. Make a joint list of all the possible ideas for evidence of learning in relation to the learning destination. Remind them that the evidence is only a record of what they have learned; it isn't – and can never be – the whole story.

Involving Students in Classroom Assessment

"Good assessment tasks are interchangeable with good instructional tasks."

Lorrie Shepard

Assessment *for* Learning

Do you want engaged, enthusiastic learners? Do you want to work with learners who strive to produce quality work? Do you want your students to learn and achieve more? The research is clear. When students are involved in the classroom assessment process, they become more engaged in learning. As mentioned earlier, the purpose of assessment is to support learning. Teachers:

1. Involve students in setting and using criteria.
2. Engage students in self-assessment.
3. Increase the sources of specific, descriptive feedback.
4. Assist students to set goals.
5. Have students collect evidence of learning in relation to standards.
6. Have students present evidence of learning in relation to standards.

Involve Students in Setting and Using Criteria

When we ask students what is important in creating a map, writing a story, doing a research report, or presenting to a small group, they get a chance to share their ideas. When teachers involve students in setting criteria, they learn more about what the students know, and students come to understand what is important while they learn. Refer to the four steps for setting and using criteria by Gregory et al. (2011a) on page 35.

1. Brainstorm a list of ideas

WHAT IS IMPORTANT FOR A QUALITY REPORT & POSTER?

- MAKES SENSE
- HAS BEGINNING, MIDDLE & END
- NEAT
- INTERESTING INFORMATION
- USE PARAGRAPHS
- INDENT
- USE DESCRIPTIVE LANGUAGE
- PUNCTUATE
- CAPITALS
- SPELLING
- ADD HUMOR, DRAMA, EMOTION
- PRACTICE READING IT OUT LOUD
- GRAB THE READER'S ATTENTION
- ADD DETAILS
- REMEMBER YOUR AUDIENCE

2. Sort and group the ideas

WHAT IS IMPORTANT FOR A QUALITY REPORT & POSTER?

☆ MAKES SENSE
☆ HAS BEGINNING, MIDDLE & END
☆ NEAT
  - INTERESTING INFORMATION
  - USE PARAGRAPHS
  - INDENT
  - USE DESCRIPTIVE LANGUAGE
  - PUNCTUATE
  - CAPITALS
☆ SPELLING
  - ADD HUMOR, DRAMA, EMOTION
☆ PRACTICE READING IT OUT LOUD
  - GRAB THE READER'S ATTENTION
  - ADD DETAILS
  - REMEMBER YOUR AUDIENCE

3. Make and post a T-Chart

CRITERIA FOR A BOOK REPORT & POSTER	SPECIFICS / DETAILS
INTERESTING TO AUDIENCE	- INTERESTING INFORMATION - USE DESCRIPTIVE LANGUAGE - ADD HUMOR, DRAMA, EMOTION - PRACTICE READING IT OUT LOUD - GRAB THE READER'S ATTENTION - ADD DETAILS - REMEMBER YOUR AUDIENCE
EASY TO FOLLOW	- MAKES SENSE - HAS BEGINNING, MIDDLE & END - USE PARAGRAPHS - SPELLING - PRACTICE READING IT OUT LOUD - NEAT
EASY TO READ	- NEAT - INDENT PARAGRAPHS - PUNCTUATE (,."*?! ETC) - CAPITALS - SPELLING - REMEMBER YOUR AUDIENCE

4. Use and revise as you learn more

CRITERIA FOR A BOOK REPORT & POSTER	SPECIFICS / DETAILS
INTERESTING TO AUDIENCE	- INTERESTING INFORMATION - USE DESCRIPTIVE LANGUAGE - PRACTICE READING IT OUT LOUD - GRAB THE READER'S ATTENTION - ADD DETAILS - REMEMBER YOUR AUDIENCE - COLOUR HELPS AUDIENCE SEE WHAT IS IMPORTANT
EASY TO FOLLOW	- MAKES SENSE - HAS BEGINNING, MIDDLE & END - USE PARAGRAPHS - SPELLING - PRACTICE READING IT OUT LOUD - NEAT - POSTER NEEDS TO LINK WORDS
EASY TO READ	- NEAT - INDENT PARAGRAPHS - PUNCTUATE (,."*?! ETC) - CAPITALS - SPELLING - REMEMBER YOUR AUDIENCE - PRINT BIG ENOUGH FOR PEOPLE TO SEE / USE LARGE FONT

This process helps keep students engaged and involved by building ownership, and helps teachers identify the needs of the group, so they can tailor the next teaching steps. Phil, a secondary school teacher who works with students who have special needs, uses the process to establish a class agreement regarding how students will act towards one another, as well as how they will go about their learning. Lisa, a kindergarten teacher, uses this process early in the year, to help students understand what is important during snack time. Debbie, teaching in a grade 7/8 classroom where every student has a laptop, asks students to talk about the important ideas when giving a slide show presentation. Consider how you might use this process - even in the early years (see examples in Chapter 7).

Engage Students in Self- and Peer Assessment

Self-assessment provides time for students to process and learn. When teachers engage students in self-assessment, they give them time to:

- process – to learn – during teaching time
- give themselves feedback
- transition from one activity or class to another

Frequent self-assessment ensures the focus stays on learning. The result is that teachers have an opportunity to find out what students are thinking and the kinds of understandings that are developing. It also allows teachers to listen to students and use their ideas as starting points for lessons. Self-assessment teaches students how to self-monitor and self-regulate, especially when it is informed by clear criteria and samples or models. Students who self-monitor are developing and practicing the skills needed to be lifelong, independent learners.

S HOW ALL STEPS
U SES CORRECT UNITS
N EAT
A CCURATE

With thanks to Laura, Winnipeg, Manitoba

It is important to co-construct criteria with students so they have a shared understanding as well as a feeling of ownership. When students share a common understanding of quality, they are better prepared to give themselves and their peers specific, descriptive feedback. One high school math class set criteria that resulted in the acronym, SUNA. When using the acronym, the students noticed that SUNA spelled backwards was a different word. The students took great delight in using that word when referring to the criteria, while the teacher always used the term, SUNA. Student ownership? Yes. Student engagement? Yes. Student learning? Yes.

The more specific, descriptive feedback students receive while they are learning, the more learning is possible. Teachers who want all students to succeed arrange ways for students to give themselves feedback or receive feedback from others. One way teachers do this is by involving students in setting criteria so they can give themselves feedback in relation to the criteria as they are working and learning. When teachers impose the criteria, no matter how clear, it is not as effective as when students help set the criteria in their own words.

A second way to increase the feedback possibilities for students is to provide models, samples or exemplars; analyze their key attributes *with* students to show what success looks like; and then ask students to use the samples, recorded demonstrations, models and exemplars to help them reach quality. Sometimes teachers demonstrate a range of quality by providing samples that show what the journey to quality looks like; other times teachers show only the best exemplars – samples which illustrate quality. The decision as to whether to show a range of samples or only high quality samples depends on the teacher's purpose for using samples. For example, writing would likely require several samples because every classroom contains a developmental range of students who need to see samples close to where they are. On the other hand, a science teacher may choose to show only outstanding science lab reports, because there is a single destination and it needs to be made very clear so that all students can be successful.

Your Name: _____
Today's Date: _____

Bless me, Ultima Presentation
Self Reflection

Respond to the following in a few sentences.

1. What was one strength of the way in which you presented your poster project (this could be one of the criteria your group focused on or another quality of a good oral presentation)?

I thought my voice was very clear and loud. This is important in making a good presentation because people have to be able to hear you when you make a presentation.

2. What is an area in which you think you need to improve during your next oral presentation review (this could be one of the criteria your group focused on or another quality of a good oral presentation)?

I think I should make better visuals because it shows how good it is.

3. What could you do in preparation to practice or develop this skill?

Practice drawing.

With thanks to Holly Tornrose, Maine

A third way teachers are arranging for students to receive more specific, descriptive feedback is by asking students to assess their peers in relation to criteria and models. As mentioned earlier, the quality of peer assessment increases when it is based on clear criteria and appropriate samples. This not only increases the amount and rate of students' learning, but can also reduce clerical time spent marking and grading.

Assist Students to Set Goals

Research and theory in neuroscience is indicating that closing in on a goal triggers a part of the brain linked to motivation. Whether you consider the often-reported Yale study where students recording their goals in writing were far more likely to achieve them, or studies related to fitness, weight loss programs or changing any habit, the trend is clearly in support of the power of goal setting. Csikszentmihalyi's (1993) research led him to write "... flow usually occurs when there are clear goals a person tries to reach, and when there is unambiguous feedback as to how well he or she is doing." Goals help bring focus and energy to bear in the service of learning. Teachers working with students know that goals become more specific and realistic when there are clear criteria and samples that show what success looks like. Goals may be short term, in that they identify next steps in the learning; or long-term, i.e., focused on improving the quality of the work – the evidence of learning – over a term or year.

Portfolio Review

Date of Review _____
Name of Reviewer _____

Two Stars

☆ YOU READ BETTER ALL THE TIME. I LIKE YOUR PATTERNS.

☆ YOU SURE KNOW A LOT ABOUT BONES. WONDERFUL DRAWING.

One Wish
TO KEEP LEARNING AND ENJOYING SCHOOL.

From Davies et al., *Together is Better*, 52

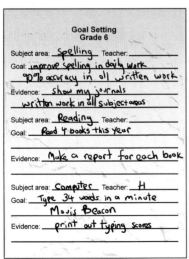

Goal Setting
Grade 6

Subject area: Spelling Teacher: _____
Goal: improve spelling in daily work 90% accuracy in all written work
Evidence: show my journals written work in all subject areas

Subject area: Reading Teacher: _____
Goal: Read 4 books this year
Evidence: Make a report for each book

Subject area: Computer Teacher: H
Goal: Type 34 words in a minute Mavis Beacon
Evidence: print out typing scores

Available as a reproducible at connect2learning.com

GOAL: I was pushing. I need to stop pushing and use words
NAME: _____

With thanks to Lisa McCluskey, Alberta

Have Students Collect Evidence of Learning

When students know what they are to learn and what it looks like to be successful, they are informed enough to self-monitor their way to success. When students collect, reflect, organize and present evidence of learning to others, they acquire skills to be more accountable for their own learning. Teachers may invite students to collect their evidence in any number of ways, from online collections to physical portfolios with a specific structure. Again, when the learning destination is clear and students have played a role in brainstorming possible evidence, they are more likely to know what needs to be collected in order for them to show proof of their learning.

Have Students Present Evidence of Learning

Audience is key to any presentation. Today's students have a variety of audiences, both in their homes and in their communities. As schools seek to be more accountable to the larger community, students are presenting their evidence of learning to a more diverse range of people, both face-to-face and online. Students who learn to present themselves as learners are more prepared to keep families and community informed and involved. Students who know

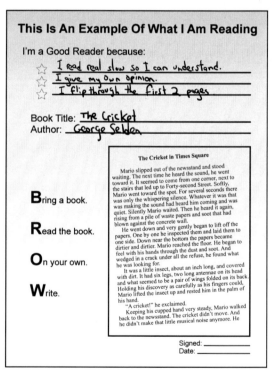

they will be providing proof of learning often assume more responsibility for collecting, reflecting on, and organizing the evidence. They are aware of what they know and can present their evidence of learning in ways appropriate to the audience, whether it is made up of their teacher(s), parents, peers, or other community members.

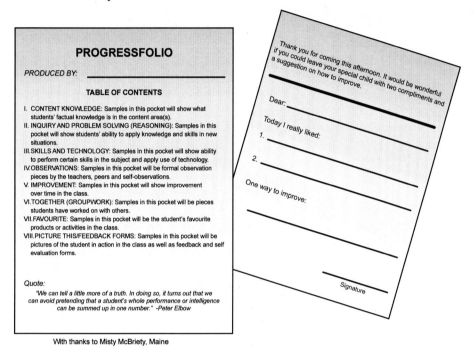

With thanks to Misty McBriety, Maine

As you consider refining and renewing your classroom assessment practices, don't be deceived by how simple it appears to be to involve students in classroom assessment. The ideas themselves are simple, but the implementing of them in today's busy classrooms will take some time. Teachers need to designate specific times for modelling, teaching, and scaffolding. Be assured that the time spent improving classroom assessment will be well worth it in terms of student learning, engagement, and achievement.

" *Holding the mind to a subject is like holding a ship to its course; it implies constant change of position combined with unity of direction.* "

John Dewey

Guiding Our Own Learning

Think about assessment in your classroom. *How does it guide instruction? How do you involve students in the process? What do you do that is similar to the ideas you have read in this chapter? What is different?* Record your thoughts.

Consider meeting with your learning circle to share ideas and strategies that work. Learning circles often find it helpful to focus on ideas related to the following topics: involving students in setting criteria, collecting samples, engaging students in peer and self-assessment, ways to collect and organize evidence, as well as ways to have students share evidence of their learning with others.

Guiding the Learning of Students

As you prepare students to assess their way to success, remember students need practice setting criteria, engaging in peer and self-assessment, and collecting and organizing evidence of their learning, as well as sharing evidence of their learning with others. Identify a starting point for you and your students. Consider co-constructing criteria around a project, a process, or a simple classroom routine, such as how to organize their notebooks for easy feedback, how to clean up or how to form a line-up. Once you have criteria that you have set together, then peer and self-assessment are more likely to be purposeful, articulate and pertinent.

Chapter 7

Using Assessment to Guide Instruction

"Assessment that works in the interests of children will enhance their ability to see and understand their learning for themselves, to judge it for themselves, and to act on their judgments."

Mary Jane Drummond

Assessment Bridges to Quality Instruction

Engaging students in assessment in the service of learning results in students both learning and learning how to learn. One reason is it teaches students how to assess their way to success. Regular involvement in classroom assessment builds a strong foundation for learning. The following examples show the assessment-learning connections across subject areas and age groups.

Classroom Clean-Up Time

Ms. M asked her Kindergarten students what they knew about keeping things clean and tidy. The students talked about helping to clean up at home and in the park.

The teacher explained that we need to keep our school tidy as well. She asked, *"What do you think is important about cleaning up in our classroom?"* The students replied, "Pick up the toys, put the books on the shelf, put the clothes back in the dress-up box, make sure the puppets are in the bin, no papers are on the floor, coats are hung up, clay and plasticine is all away, all puzzle pieces are in the right box, Lego in the Lego centre box, sand toys in the sand box."

The teacher recorded all the contributions on sentence strips. Then she said, *"When we clean up today, I want you to notice what else you do."* When they were finished, she asked them what else had been part of cleanup. One child said, "Everyone is supposed to help." Another said, "We can't make lots of noise." "And we have to hurry," said another. "Yeah," said a student, "or we'll miss the bus." The teacher recorded all their additional comments.

Before cleanup time the next day, the teacher read their list to them. Halfway through cleanup she called them to the group meeting area and said, *"Let's think about how we are doing with cleanup. As I read the list again, make the thumbs-up sign if you think you are helping in that way."* The students listened and put their thumbs up for different items. When she had completed the list, the teacher reminded the class about the paint centre and asked them to think about one thing they were going to do to help clean up that area. She also asked them to whisper it to a neighbour, and then they returned to their task.

Several days later, the class reviewed the list again after cleanup time. The teacher said, *"Our brains have a difficult time remembering all these things. I think we could group them in this way."* She moved the strips into groups under the following labels:
- **W**orking Together
- **E**verything in Its Place
- **T**hinking and Acting Safely

The acronym to remind the class was WET. It became part of the daily routine for the students to self-assess at the end of cleanup time. The teacher would ask, *"Are we all WET? Did we work together?" Is everything in its place? Did we think and act safely?"*

> **What's important about cleanup time?**
>
> Pick up the toys
> Put the books on the shelf
> Put the clothes back in the dress-up box
> Make sure the puppets are in the bin
> No papers on the floor
> Coats are hung up
> Clay and plasticine is all away
> Puzzle pieces are all in the right box
> Lego in the lego centre box
> Sand toys in the sand box

Reading Aloud to Others

Mr. F wanted his primary students to focus on oral reading strategies. He began by asking, *"What is important when we read out loud?"* As the class talked together, they created the following list:

- You can hear their voice easily
- They show the pictures
- Your voice goes up and down
- If the book has a question, your voice has a question in it
- Read with expression
- You hold the book so they can see your face
- You practice first
- If you get stuck, you can stop and ask for help
- Read to someone you want to read to

As students in the class read their practiced passages aloud during Reading Club time, the teacher encouraged them to listen and to compliment each other. The compliments they gave reflected the reader's performance and the listener's understanding of what a good oral reading performance sounds like. Students made comments such as, "You used really good expression," "I liked the way your voice went low when you read the giant's part," or "I liked the way you took a breath at the end of the sentence." If the compliment lacked specificity, such as "It was good" or "You did a good job," the teacher would follow up by asking, *"What made it good?"* It quickly became a class expectation that compliments would be specific, so the person receiving them would know exactly what he or she had done well.

After they had practiced giving compliments, the teacher asked if there was anything else they had noticed about what good readers do when they read out loud. One child said that his dad had said to take a break and breathe in when you get to a period. The children discussed this and agreed that that was another thing they did sometimes. After this discussion, the teacher used the students' ideas to make up a recording sheet. Students used the sheet when they read in partners.

The teacher gave students copies of the recording sheet and explained how to use it with a partner. One person would read while the other person would listen and check off everything that she or he saw or heard the reader doing. Then they would change places.

Reading Aloud
Reader's Name: _____
Supporter's Name: _____
As you listen to your partner read, notice the things he or she does that show she or he reads well to others.
☐ You can hear the reader's voice easily.
☐ The reader shows the pictures.
☐ The reader's voice goes up and down (has expression).
☐ If the book has a question, the reader's voice has a question in it.
☐ The reader holds the book so you can see his or her face.
☐ The reader practises first so she or he knows most of the words.
☐ If the reader gets stuck, he or she stops and asks for help.
☐ _____
☐ _____

Adapted from Politano and Davies, *Multi-Age and More*, 88

The teacher read a story, and the class practiced using the recording sheet by listening to the things he did that showed he was a good reader. Then they worked with partners and practiced reading aloud. When they were ready, they used the sheet to record observations about each other's reading. As their skills increased, they added more ideas to the list and began to set goals – each student focusing on one thing they were trying to do better. Before starting to read, the student would ask the observer to watch for evidence of the goal. This became a routine way for students to give each other descriptive feedback. The record sheets went into their assessment boxes as evidence.

Research Project

Mrs. C's students were asked to research in relation to a question they identified and then find a way to effectively communicate what they had learned. As they began their projects, Mrs. C gave a series of mini-lessons to teach them about the research process. She conferenced with different groups of students who were experiencing similar difficulties. The students thought about how they were going to show what they had learned through their research. When they had made their choices in this area, she decided that they were ready to set criteria for an effective research project. She began by having them brainstorm a list entitled, "What Is Important in a Research Project?" This is part of the list they created:

- pictures
- on topic
- keeps people paying attention
- correct spelling
- interesting sentences
- has beginning, middle, and end
- keep in a safe place
- good describing words
- punctuation (. , ! ? " " ….)
- interesting ideas
- tells what is important

The teacher added three other details to the list:
- the form selected helps to communicate the information clearly
- uses at least three sources
- has a bibliography

Once all the ideas were listed, the class sorted them and made a T-chart. The criteria were:
- organized so audience can follow
- has interesting information
- keeps audience interested and attending
- edited so audience can understand easily

The T-chart was photocopied for each student. Their first task was to highlight each word or phrase that was true for their project at this point. If they felt they had completely met any of the criteria on the left, they were to write "Met" and provide evidence by highlighting "Proof" in their report. For the criteria they had not yet met, they were asked to circle one or two details that they were going to work on, and then make a plan for their next steps. They shared their work plans with partners and then set to work. The process of setting criteria and making the end product more clear helped them see where they were in

Research Project

Criteria	Details
Organized So Audience Can Follow	- has beginning, middle and end - keep in a safe place - tells what is important - has a bibliography
Has Interesting Information	- not boring (exciting) - lots of information - brainstorm / web - different sources, like the Internet - sign language, skits, props - uses at least three sources
Keeps Audience Interested and Attending	- pictures, sign language - on topic - keeps people paying attention - could be power point presentation
Edited So Audience Can Understand Easily	- good describing words - punctuation (. , ! ? " " ....) - indented paragraphs - correct spelling - interesting sentences - the form selected helps to communicate the information clearly

relation to where they needed to be. While most students worked towards meeting all the criteria, two students with special needs, in consultation with the learning resource teacher and after looking at their Individual Education Plans (IEP), chose one of the four criteria to focus on during this project.

Science Labs

Mr. H used a selection of samples to help prepare his students for writing science lab reports. He selected samples from previous years that were good quality models of the required features. He made two copies of each science lab report, so he had eight samples. He gave one sample to each group of three or four students. They analyzed one sample and then traded and analyzed a second and a third. As they looked at the samples, each group made a list of what makes a really good science lab report. After they had had enough time to look at a few samples, the class compiled a whole-class list of criteria. The teacher added two things students hadn't noticed. All the brainstormed ideas were grouped and used to create a T-chart that was posted in the class. The criteria were listed on the left side, and the details that the class had brainstormed were listed on the right side. The three criteria the class developed were: scientific method is complete and easy to follow; data are accurately presented and interpreted; and conclusion(s) is/are valid.

Science Lab Criteria for report	Met	Not Yet Met	Please notice...
Scientific method is complete and easy to follow	✓		I rewrote this twice
Data are accurately presented and interpreted	✓		notice the details in my diagram and I also included a chart this time
Conclusion(s) is valid	✓		

Conference requested ☐   Question(s):

Date(s) received: Oct. 16

Assessed by ☐ teacher ☑ self ☐ partner ☐ other

Assignment: Science Lab #4

Student: Aaron D. Block C

Adapted from Gregory, Cameron and Davies, *Self-Assessment and Goal Setting*, 2nd Edition

The students wrote up their first lab report using the samples as models. Before handing in their reports, the teacher asked them to self-assess, noting which criteria had been met, which were not yet met, and what they wanted the teacher to notice when he assessed their lab reports. He reminded them to show in the lab report itself where the evidence was located. Before doing the next science lab report, they reviewed the previous report with the criteria in mind and selected one thing to improve.

Mathematics

Mrs. J's description for success guides her teaching and classroom assessment. She has a growing collection of work samples to show quality. The samples and the description are used to help students understand success, to assign grades for report cards and to document student learning as part of the school's local assessment. Early in the term, she shares the learning goals and with the students, brainstorms a list of possible evidence or proof of their learning. Periodically, she has them identify the current best pieces of evidence. Prior to the mid-term and final reports, she meets briefly with students to review their strengths and areas needing improvement, and to set goals. The ongoing evidence of learning includes:

Grade 7 - Learning Results	Description of Success	Evidence of Learning
Students will:	**Students can:**	**Evidence includes:**
Understand and demonstrate a sense of what numbers mean and how they are used.	Create and interpret bar and line graphs including collections of raw data.	Notebooks Projects Tests Quizzes Geometry projects
Understand that mathematics is the science of patterns, relationships, and functions.	Name, create and find the area and circumference of a variety of geometric shapes.	Graphs and charts Data analysis project Completed word problems Work sheets Math journals
Understand and demonstrate computation and measurement skills.	Calculate mean, median, mode, and range data. Calculate percentages, decimals, and fractions.	Constructed responses Emails Website collection Inspiration web
Understand and apply concepts from geometry and algebra.	Use exponents and scientific notation.	
Understand and apply concepts in discrete mathematics and mathematical reasoning (problem solving).	Understand basic units of measure in the metric system. Solve a basic 3 step equation.	
Reflect upon and clarify their understanding of mathematical ideas and relationships.	Write and solve word problems. Use a number line to calculate negative numbers. Read and use a protractor and compass.	

- *Observations:* notes, interviews, checklists, and records (e.g., work completion, practice work, and homework)
- *Products:* Math notebooks, papers, projects, performance tasks, quizzes, revisions, pre- and post-tests, and yearly pre-assessment
- *Conversations:* small and large group conversations, homework debriefings, board work, peer tutoring, and self-assessment in relation to criteria

The evidence of learning used for the local assessment includes two performance tasks, student self-assessment in relation to criteria, as well as a comparison to student work completed during the school year.

In the Specialist Classroom

Ms. M teaches choir twice a week for 30 minutes to elementary school students. She begins the year by talking about what is important when singing in a choir. She also explains to students that she and other people who listen to the choir will be judging their singing just like the judges on television shows. She works with the students to brainstorm all their ideas about what the judges need to look for in a choir performance. They build the list over the first few weeks of school, adding to it as they think of more ideas. The students practice their singing. Sometimes they watch and listen to great choirs. Sometimes they watch videos of their own choir performances. They analyze the performances, debrief what they have seen and heard, and continue to add to the list of what makes a great choir performance. Once the list is comprehensive, Ms. M works with students to sort the ideas and build a T-chart. The resulting criteria on the T-chart guide their ongoing learning, assessment and evaluation.

Collecting Evidence of Learning at Post-Secondary

Students at all levels benefit from the kind of assessment practices described in this book. The same techniques can be used effectively in post-secondary classrooms. During a course, students are responsible for collecting and organizing evidence of their learning in relation to the course goals, and for finalizing the collection at the end of the course. A self-assessment sheet demonstrates one way to help them collect and organize their evidence.

Criteria for Excellence in this Course	Details / Specifics	Please Notice...
Submits Quality Products	- unique - publishable / distributable - well-articulated - meets audience's needs - concise	I have included evidence in each pocket that addresses the learning outcomes and meets the criteria for excellence (at least I think so!). I have also tried to triangulate the evidence in each pocket - I'm not sure I have enough. Please give me feedback on this - and anything else where I am off track.
Makes Personal and Theoretical Connections to Theory and Research	- deep and insightful understanding of research and practice - gives examples - uses analogy / metaphor	
Extends Thinking of Self and Others	- contributes to all our learning - evidence of extensive reading - relevant ideas - thoughtful connections and questions	

The Big Picture

The examples in this chapter illustrate how instruction is changing as we involve students in classroom assessment. By engaging students in the process of linking to prior knowledge, describing success, setting criteria, self-assessing, giving feedback, setting goals, and collecting and presenting evidence of their own learning, educators are teaching students *how to learn* as well as teaching them what they need to know and be able to do.

If the ideas in this chapter are new to you, take your time to learn more before implementing them in your classroom. Seek resources that give you classroom-tested ideas and connect with colleagues who are also trying to involve students more in assessment. Consider starting with one technique and taking the time needed to transform it from idea to habit. Consider choosing one thing to *stop* doing – maybe some of that evaluative marking and grading – in order to have time to do the new thing.

However you choose to refine your current teaching and assessment practices, remember to adapt the ideas to make them work with your students in your school community. Remember, the person working the hardest is likely to be learning the most. *Isn't it time your students worked harder than you?*

"*We can make trains run on time, but if they do not go where we want them to go, why bother?***"**

Neil Postman

Guiding Our Own Learning

Think about a time when students in your classroom were most engaged in learning. Reflect on the following questions:

- What was happening? What were they doing?
- Where were you? What were you doing?
- Did students know the learning destination?
- Did they know what was expected of them in terms of doing the learning?
- Did they know what kind of evidence they would need to produce?
- Were they able to self-monitor in relation to models, criteria and/or samples?

Record your thoughts.

Guiding the Learning of Students

Ask students to build a list of criteria in response to the question: *What do good teachers do that supports your learning?* Listen and reflect on their responses in terms of your own teaching.

Collecting, Organizing, and Presenting Evidence

" " *The student knows more than the teacher about what and how he has learned – even if he knows less about what was taught.* **" "**

Peter Elbow

Collecting, organizing, and presenting evidence of learning used to be the teacher's responsibility alone. If students are to be involved in assessment *in support of* their learning, then they must also be involved in this crucial aspect. Part of learning is recognizing when you've succeeded. You know you've succeeded when you see the evidence. Learners need to collect and organize their evidence, in relation to the learning destination, so they know that they are learning. They need to present their evidence so that others will be able to verify they are learning. That's what it means to be accountable. It is also part of the pathway to self-regulation.

To have all the evidence we need for balanced and fair assessment, it isn't enough that teachers review work once, record the grade or score and the file, or send the work home. Instead, students need to be involved in gathering and creating comprehensive collections of evidence over a period of time – that is, products, self-assessments, and recorded observations. The student's collection of evidence becomes a visual history of her or his learning over time. Both the collection itself and the process of creating it are valuable in several ways.

Chapter 8

Contents

- Gathering and making sense of collections of evidence helps students to learn and practice organizational skills, to take pride in their work, and to discover their own learning styles. Developing skills to collect evidence and present themselves and their learning to others prepares students for life.

- Students' collections of evidence help improve the quality and specificity of communications between teachers, students, and parents. Showing collections of evidence to parents helps demystify the learning process and provides the information they need to be partners in assessment.

- Students can use their collections to show teachers and parents what they know and what they need to learn. This process helps students better understand their own learning and their progress It provides opportunities to represent learning in a variety of ways. It also helps to verify the learning.

- Because collections of evidence help students and parents recognize progress for themselves, they are a rich resource for reporting. They enlarge the view of what has been learned, provide a window into student thinking, and give a multi-dimensional view of the student as a learner. The more extensive the collection of evidence, the better view it gives of the student's abilities. A range of evidence collected over time and across different tasks increases the validity and reliability of the assessment and evaluation for everyone.

Making the Process Work

There are four keys to ensuring that collecting and organizing evidence supports student learning in your classroom:

1. Keep the process simple.
2. Involve students.
3. Help students and parents value the evidence.
4. Reconsider evidence collections.

Keep the process simple

The process of students collecting evidence of learning needs to be practical and possible. As the challenge of helping students learn becomes more and more complex, our routines and system of collecting evidence must be simplified to take the minimum amount of time to maintain.

Here are some points to keep in mind when designing a process:

- Help students understand *why* they are keeping track of their evidence.
- Explain *who* is going to see the evidence.
- Work with students to design a *simple system* that they can use (e.g., folders or magazine files, physical or digital storage).
- Provide students with *time* to to collect, select, and store their evidence.

How you choose to have students involved in representing, collecting and organizing evidence depends on many factors, such as digital resources available, physical space, the age of your students, and whether you teach one class or several. In asking students to represent what they know in a variety of ways, the evidence is expanding beyond "paper and pencil." Since bulky evidence, such as a stage set or physical models of places, take too much space in the classroom, they must be represented in different forms. Work with students to figure out how the evidence can be recorded in another way, such as through photographs, slide show, video, audio, shared via an app, or some other digital option. Records of learning such as these help capture the evidence that otherwise might be forgotten.

To keep the evidence safe, have storage systems such as folders, boxes, or bins in the classroom. If the evidence is in digital form make sure regular back-ups are made and that both teacher and student have access to the evidence online through tools such as Google Docs and Dropbox. When a system for organizing the physical evidence is in place, plan to give students time to add to the collection of evidence on a regular basis. Have students keep as much evidence as they can – you never know what might be important later. Storage can be simplified if bulky items are sent home after digital photographs are taken and self-assessments are completed. Performances, both formal and informal, can also be recorded in a digital format. In addition to students' collections, teachers need to collect their own observation notes and evidence for later evaluation. Sometimes students simply date and file the evidence, knowing they will sort it later. In some classrooms, students have sufficient access to technology to allow all evidence that is kept to be stored in digital form. Systems for reminding us to back-up digital evidence are essential.

There are many ways that teachers and students can choose to collect, organize, and present evidence. Here are just a few examples.

Ms. M's early primary students collect their work in notebooks, personal magazine file boxes, and progress portfolios.

Mr. S's intermediate students have file drawers in which they store loose papers, their binders, and portfolios for which they select entries each Friday. They share student work online using a work share app.

Ms. R's Grade 8 students have progress portfolios, back-and-forth work folders, and fat folders. The paper-based evidence is in fat folders which are stored in thin plastic crates near her desk. Digital materials are stored in digital folders.

Mr. D's students use a software application to organize their daily work. Each subject's learning outcomes (or standards) are grouped. Then, each digital item of evidence of learning is attached and stored. Students make different selections as their proof of learning changes over time.

Ms. G's Grade 9 students have writing folders, notebooks, and other folders on their digital desktop from which they select work to show how they are learning over time.

Mr. C teaches university students. His students collect and store the evidence online in a shared learning space so they have access for feedback, direction, and final collections of evidence. Their decision-making process is guided by the detailed description of what kind of evidence is required. He also involves students in co-constructing criteria for each assignment and encourages them to resubmit assignments up until the end of the course.

Ms. T's students post their work online on the school's server. Students invite parents and others to sign in and review the work, post comments, and see growth over time.

Involve students

Students need to be accountable for their learning – it helps us and it helps them. When students are responsible for assembling the evidence, they have more opportunities to figure out whether they are on track with their learning. It is the teacher's job to show them how to do it well.

Involve students in planning for success by reviewing the learning destination and asking them what proof of learning they need in order to be organized, monitor their progress, and later, to account for their learning. Be clear about what evidence is essential and where students have flexibility to show what they know in a variety of ways.

Some teachers arrange time on a regular basis so students can record what the evidence represents and what they want the viewer to notice. Having students explain their thinking - using self-assessment (written or recorded) - helps them come to know themselves better as learners. Their involvement in setting and using criteria around key aspects of the evidence helps them articulate their learning. They learn the language of assessment.

When parents or others view the evidence, read or listen to the digital notes that the students have made, and discuss their learning as they look through the evidence, they gain insights into what has been learned and what still needs to be learned.

Windham Middle School
Portfolio Entry Slip

Name: _____   Grade: _7_

Teacher: _____

Title: Reading Reflection   Date Completed: _____

My entry shows evidence in the following guiding principle(s)

I.   A clear and effective communicator
II. A self-directed and lifelong learner
III. A creative and practical problem solver
IV. A responsible and involved citizen
V.   A collaborative and quality worker
VI. An integrative and informed thinker

Describe the assignment:
For this assignment I had to:
· choose a page of my current independent reading book
· tell why I am a good reader
· record author, title, date, + signature

This work shows I learned:
That mostly I get a image inside my head when I am reading a great book. But if I don't get a good book then I don't get a image, because the book isn't really interesting.

This work was done (please check appropriate comment):

✓ In Class   _ As Homework   _ With Teacher Feedback
_ In a group   ✓ Alone   _ With Peer Feedback
_ As a First Draft Only   _ With revision   ✓ Other conditions (explain)
                                              my feedback

With thanks to Windham Middle School, Maine
Available as a reproducible at connect2learning.com

Help parents and students value the evidence

Building collections of evidence usually means that only some student work goes home, while the rest stays at school, so that it is on hand for review and discussion. Your parents may want to see more to plan ahead to address their needs. Sometimes students take home weekly files of work and then bring them back after parents have viewed them. Sometimes students store almost all evidence at school. Students in technology-rich settings create digital collections of evidence that can be accessed at anytime online.

When students bring their work home, sometimes parents don't understand what the samples show in terms of student learning. Help students be prepared to explain. You might have students write notes pointing out why the evidence is important and where it can be viewed. Once school has been in session for a while, the class might invite parents to an afternoon open house to view the evidence; students might prepare for and then conduct an out-of-school conference with their parents or other audiences; or students might give parents a tour of their class or personal website.

Dear Parents:

As you look through your child's work, please notice, as I have, the areas he or she has had success with and the things he or she needs to improve.

While I have assessed all the work in this collection, I have chosen to place a grade or write a note about only some of the work. You will know I have assessed the work when you see a score, a comment, a checkmark or my initials.

If you have any questions about your child's learning, I would be pleased to discuss it with you. Please call me and we can arrange a time to talk.

Best wishes,

Mr. Taylor

As you increase the amount of descriptive feedback and decrease the amount of evaluative feedback, you may not be marking or grading work in ways parents expect. Let parents know that you are continuing to assess all student work, although you may not be responding with a mark or grade. A note such as the one shown here on the left helps to explain your approach and alleviate parent concerns.

Reconsidering Evidence Collections

When students present their work to others, they share all or part of the evidence they have been collecting. These can include any evidence the student has created, such as notebooks, projects, assignments, performances, quizzes and tests. They may be print, video, or audio and stored in analogue or digital form. A collection of evidence that has a purpose and an audience is often called a portfolio. Portfolios can have a variety of purposes, some of which are to show progress, to show process, to show "best work," to show evidence of learning in relation to the learning destination, or to show evidence of meeting goals – or a combination of purposes to fit the needs of a particular audience.

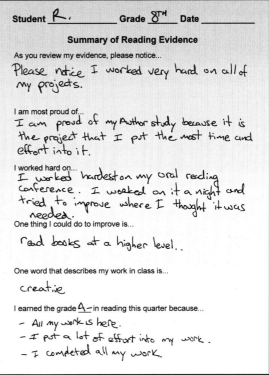

Student **R.**   Grade **8TH**   Date _____

Summary of Reading Evidence

As you review my evidence, please notice...
Please notice I worked very hard on all of my projects.

I am most proud of...
I am proud of my Author study because it is the project that I put the most time and effort into it.

I worked hard on...
I worked hardest on my oral reading conference. I worked on it a night and tried to improve where I thought it was needed.

One thing I could do to improve is...
read books at a higher level..

One word that describes my work in class is...
creative

I earned the grade A– in reading this quarter because...
- All my work is here.
- I put a lot of effort into my work.
- I completed all my work.

With thanks to Pearl Butler, Maine
Available as a reproducible at connect2learning.com

Portfolios

In *Collecting Evidence and Portfolios: Engaging Students in Pedagogical Documentation* (Davies, Herbst, and Augusta 2017), the authors write, "There are many ways students and teachers can collect evidence of learning. For example:
- Students select a piece of work from the week to prove that they've met a content standard.
- Students place work samples in a fat folder or in a desktop folder.

Semester 1: What does my portfolio show about my work in this class?	Name: _____ Date: _____

List of Evidence - Check off what's in each pocket	**Strengths, Areas of Growth, and Areas to Work On**
Reading Pocket: ✓ House on Mango Street Test ✓ Bless Me Ultima Quiz 1 ✓ Bless Me Ultima Quiz 2 ✓ Bless Me Ultima Poster	What does your work in this area of class show about your skills in reading comprehension and literary analysis? STRENGTH: I AM ABLE TO ANALYZE READING BASED ON WHAT HAS BEEN DISCUSSED IN CLASS AND MY OWN INTERPRETATIONS. GROWTH: I'M MAKING MORE CONCISE ARGUMENTS VS. HAVING LONG & DRAWN OUT EXPLANATIONS. WORK ON: I NEED TO READ DIRECTIONS & CONTEXT MORE CAREFULLY SO I CAN PROPERLY IDENTIFY THINGS (IE. FIGURATIVE LANGUAGE)
Writing Pocket: ✓ Summer Reading Book Review ✓ Vignette Collection ✓ Quote Reflection # 1 ✓ Resume	What does your work in this area of class show about your skills in writing for a variety of purposes and using standard English conventions? STRENGTH: MY SEC IS VERY GOOD AND I DON'T THINK I'VE HAD A RUNON OR A FRAGMENT YET. GROWTH: I AM MORE AWARE OF WHAT THE COMMA RULES ARE COMPARED TO LAST YEAR SO I CAN ACCEPTABLY SELF-EDIT WORK ON: I NEED TO DO A BETTER JOB OF PROOF READING → LOOKING FOR WORDS THAT MAY BE SPELLED CORRECTLY BUT DON'T MAKE SENSE TO WHAT I'M SAYING.
Speaking Pocket: ✓ Book Review Presentation ✓ Bless Me Ultima Poster Sharing	What does your work in this area of class show about your skills in speaking in front of others? STRENGTH: I MAINTAIN EYE CONTACT WITH MY LISTENERS & DON'T FIDGET SO PEOPLE KNOW I AM WELL PREPARED AND SERIOUS. GROWTH: I ADJUST VOICE TONE TO THE SIZE OF THE GROUP & BASED ON IF THERE ARE MULTIPLE PRESENTATIONS. WORK ON: I NEED TO SPEAK SLOWER SO MY INFORMATION IS BETTER RECIEVED.
Learning Pocket: ✓ Multiple Intelligences Self Assessment ✓ Reading Activities Brainstorm ✓ Progress Report Q1 and Self Reflection (Oct. 8) ✓ End of Q1 Summary and Self Reflection (Nov. 1) ✓ Progress Report Q2 and Self Reflection (Dec. 10)	Looking back through your reflections, progress reports, and quarter 1 summary, what trends or patterns do you see in your work habits? I SEE THAT I AM CONSISTANT IN GETTING MY WORK DONE AND DOING IT WELL. I ALSO MENTIONED ON MY REFLECTIONS THAT I WANT TO KNOW MORE GRAMMAR. What relationship or correlation do you see between your progress in the skills of this class and your work habits? I THINK THAT SOME OF MY WRITING IS BECOMING A BIT MORE CONCISE AND IS LEAVING OUT SOME UNNEEDED INFORMATION. MY WORK HABITS ARE ALSO IMPROVING BECAUSE I AM MORE FOCUSED AND AM GETTING WORK DONE BETTER & FASTER. How did you do in meeting the goals you set for Q2 on your Q1 reflection? (on back) YES, I'VE MET MY GOALS OR HAVE BEGUN TO BECAUSE I'M PARTICIPATING MORE IN CLASS & AM HAVING NOT AS MANY SEC ERRORS.
Setting Goals for Third Quarter **Based on what needs you saw in your work, set three goals for Quarter 3 in each main area of class**	**Reading -** I'M GOING TO READ DIRECTIONS/QUESTIONS AT LEAST ONCE BEFORE DOING A TASK SO I DO IT COMPLETELY & DON'T ACCIDENTLY LEAVE SOMETHING OUT. **Writing -** I'M GOING TO PROOF READ MY WORK BETTER SO THAT I CAN CORRECT WORDS WHICH HAVE BEEN LEFT OUT OF WORDS THAT DON'T MAKE SENSE IN CONTEXT. **Speaking -** WHEN GIVING A PRESENTATION I WILL SPEAK SLOWER WHICH MEANS PREPARING MORE SO I WON'T RUSH TO THE FINISH.

Caroline, The specificity of this reflection should set you up for a strong Q3 + a lot of growth over this year. Excellent insights. Mrs Tornrose

With thanks to Holly Tornrose, Maine

- Teachers insert into an electronic application (like Seesaw) a short video clip of math manipulatives being used to solve a math problem.
- Students select one piece of work and attach a proof card to show their learning (Gregory, Cameron, and Davies 2011b, pp. 30-32).
- Students write about what's going on in an image that has been taken of them engaged in learning (Gregory, Cameron, and Davies 2011c, p. 27).
- Students show evidence of meeting criteria as they solve problems in Mathematics by using colour-coded sticky notes.
- Students select a piece of work to put into their goal envelope (Gregory, Cameron, and Davies 2011c, pp. 23-24).
- Students write the words they remember from the learning of the week.
- Teachers ask students to use an application like Pro-Create to sketch, paint and, create an image to visually represent the concepts studied in a biology unit.
- Teachers ask young students to record their "think alouds" when they are solving a mathematics problem using an electronic application (e.g., applications such as Educreations, ShowMe, or Explain Everything).

This list of possibilities can, in fact, be endless. Some ways to gather evidence for portfolios take a few minutes, while others are more complex and involve a variety of steps and take place over a longer period of time.

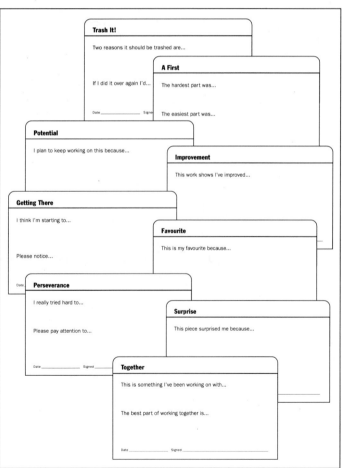

Adapted from Gregory, Cameron, and Davies, *Self-Assessment and Goal Setting*, 2nd Edition, 32.

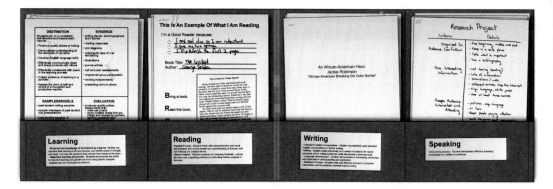

Students and teachers can be jointly responsible for pedagogically documenting evidence of learning. Structures include:

1. Achievement Portfolio
2. Competencies Portfolio
3. Progression Portfolio
4. Growth Portfolio
5. Pathway Portfolio

Though the content and form of the portfolio or collection of evidence can be negotiated by and with the students, including portfolios and collections of evidence is not negotiable. This is a way by which students have an active and primary role in the assessment process and in pedagogical documentation." (pp. 24-26).

Research Connection:

Research shows that when students are involved in the assessment process—by co-constructing the criteria by which they are assessed, self-assessing in relation to the criteria, giving themselves information to guide (or "feed-forward") their learning, collecting and presenting evidence of their learning, and reflecting on their strengths and needs—they learn more, achieve at higher levels, and are more motivated. They are also better able to set informed, appropriate learning goals to further improve their learning. (Black and Wiliam 1998, 2018; Crooks 1988; Davies 2004; Stiggins 2007)

You can learn more practical ways to select and implement portfolios and collections of evidence in *Collecting Evidence and Portfolios: Engaging Students in Pedagogical Documentation* (Davies, Herbst, and Augusta 2017).

Taking the Time

It takes time to support students as they assume a larger role in collecting their own assessment evidence. It is time worth taking because students have an opportunity to become more responsible and involved in their own learning and, as a result, learn more. It is also worthwhile because students know their audience (their parents, family members and teacher) and what evidence their audience needs to help them understand and appreciate the learning. Receiving feedback from people whose opinion they value can increase not only students' motivation but also their learning.

As teachers we decide the balance of teacher work and student involvement that is comfortable for us – there is no right or wrong way. The balance between teacher work and student work will vary from year to year. As you make your choices, remember that *the person who is working the hardest is learning the most.*

" *Life is complex. Each one of us must make his own path through life. There are no self-help manuals, no formulas, no easy answers. The right road for one is the wrong road for another... The journey of life is not paved in blacktop; it is not brightly lit, and it has no road signs. It is a rocky path through the wilderness.* "

M. Scott Peck

Guiding Our Own Learning

Ask your colleagues how their students are involved in organizing and collecting evidence of their learning in relation to standards or outcomes. Listen for ideas that might help you, as well as ways to make it easier to involve students. Record the ideas.

Think about the evidence your students need to produce and what you want the audience to learn about as they view the evidence collection. Record your thoughts. Consider them as you design the ways your students will collect, reflect, and share their learning with others. Once your plan is complete, put it into action.

Guiding the Learning of Students

Continue to involve students in assessing for success:
- Ask students to collect evidence of learning in relation to one unit of study. Remind them that different students may have different kinds of proof, depending on how they choose to show what they've been learning.
- Periodically, ask students to find proof of meeting one standard or learning outcome and record why they feel their evidence is proof.
- Encourage students to use the language of the criteria you set together to guide their self- and peer assessment.

Communicating About Learning

❝ … we can tell a little more of the truth. In doing so, it turns out that we can avoid pretending that a student's whole performance or intelligence can be summed up in one number. ❞

Peter Elbow

In the past, informal communications – such as conversations in the parking lot, by the boot racks, in the local market or on the lanai, as well as notes or a telephone call to the parents – helped build partnerships between home and school. Casual communications such as these kept students, their families, and teachers in step with each other.

As family life grows busier and more complex, and the information glut overwhelms even the most organized of us, we feel we have less time to become informed. Adding to the challenge is the increasing diversity and changing values of our communities. Sometimes, while we might wonder, there is a common meeting place. It is essential we provide opportunities for families, schools, and teachers to come together in caring about the students. We all want the best for each one of them, even though we may express it in different ways.

Successful Communications

One solution to the challenge of finding ways to communicate is through involving students. When students communicate with others about their learning, they come to understand what they have learned, what they need to learn, and what kind of support may be available to them. They receive feedback and recognition from themselves and from others that guide and support their learning. The process of preparing and presenting gives students an opportunity to construct their understanding and to help others make meaning of their learning. This teaches them to self-monitor – an essential skill for self-directed, independent, lifelong learners.

When parents and others watch demonstrations of learning or attend student-parent conferences, it increases their appreciation of their son or daughter as a learner, his or her level of skill development, the breadth of the classroom and school curriculum, and the efforts needed on everyone's behalf to make learning possible. When the audience is invited to respond, they acknowledge and support the learning, while giving students valuable feedback.

There are two parts to successful communication about learning:

1. Students collect and demonstrate their learning.
2. Audiences respond with feedback.

Students Collect and Demonstrate Their Learning

When students are involved in preparing and organizing the communication for a specific audience, the message is more likely to be understood. Often, these days, students act as translator and interpreter in order to bridge school and home. This is partly because students themselves have a good idea about the best way to communicate with different audiences. These may be made up of parents, family members, family friends, students in another class, or members of the community. Having a specific audience helps focus the presentation, making it more purposeful and likely to inform.

Teachers develop ways for students to communicate about their learning that work for the students, the parents, and the school community. For example, one class invited their parents for an open house, and the students explained their classroom program using Readers' Theatre (Nye 1999). Another class invited parents to view online portfolios (Sueoko 2013). These days there are numerous communication apps that facilitate ongoing information-sharing online. As teachers, we need to continually update our use of digital communication tools in order to stay connected.

When students are actively engaged in communicating evidence of their learning to their families, the teacher's role changes from doing the communicating to guiding the process and organizing students, who then show or demonstrate their own learning. Other communication methods make use of student-generated newsletters, student self-assessments and work samples, demonstrations of learning at home or at school, and student-parent conferences.

Team Bushido Community Expectation	What I did/Please look at...
1. Be responsible for learning	I listened when teacher was talking + I do my homework
2. Understand it is essential for people to work together	I cooperate + help my group for help. If I didn't or the group didn't it would have been difficult
3. Be involved in complex thinking and problem solving	I helped problem solve what to make out of a number of materials
4. Be able to recognize and produce quality products and quality performances	I think I showed it with my invention convention. I did a good job. I had fun + worked hard

Teacher Comments _____
_____
_____

I am especially proud of _My invention convention. I worked hard + I thought my invention was the best!_
_____

I would like to work on _not asking the teacher so often for help. Ask him/her to please explain better so I understand better._
_____

Parent/Guardian Comments _____
_____
_____

_____
Student Signature

Student-generated newsletters

Student-generated newsletters provide parents with information about the classroom program as well as student learning. Students work individually or in small groups to take responsibility for communicating about the daily learning taking place in their classrooms. Creating the newsletter is a valuable experience for students, giving them a real purpose and audience for their efforts. It requires them to collect evidence and articulate their learning in ways that make sense to others.

Self-assessments and work samples

Teachers ask students to think about and reflect on their work because it helps students learn. The self-assessments become a valuable way for them to communicate with their parents about learning. These traditionally included samples of student work sent home for parent review, such as two math work samples showing progress; a portfolio showing best work; a photograph of the student at work, with an explanation of what the student is learning about; or a video that records students performing. Student self-assessments and accompanying work samples are selected to show a range that allows parents to see the breadth of classroom work beyond "paper and pencil" evidence. These days applications such as Seesaw, Fresh Grade, and more are in common use.

Such communications keep parents informed and help students realize that others care about their learning. Using sentence starters can guide parent and family responses to students resulting in more feedback for learning while helping teachers understand what the audience values and what questions there might be.

Demonstrations of learning

Sometimes an effective way for students to show parents what they've learned is through demonstrations that take place at home, at school or online. Students may take home a math game, the materials for a science experiment, a musical instrument, a videotaped performance, a book to read aloud, or a web-based activity, and invite parents to respond.

This weekend for outdoor education I went surf kayaking in the ocean. It was really hard at first, but when I figured out how to roll back up when I flipped, it made the weekend a lot more fun. That also helped me keep out of the cold water so I could stay out longer.

P.S. My friend Alison Kakish took this photo.

Adapted from Gregory, Cameron and Davies, *Conferencing and Reporting,* 2001, 2011

Sometimes a classroom teacher will organize a demonstration of learning to take place at school or through the school online communication application. This may include family subject-focused activities, such as: a Math Night where children teach parents math games in the library; student-parent conferences where students show parents and extended family members their portfolios or collections of schoolwork; science laboratory experiments conducted by students for parents in the lab; exhibits of students' posted work samples; or online forums with posted work.

Most schools have some way to involve students in demonstrating their learning during the year. Schools plan events such as seasonal music concerts, drama performances, track meets, fine arts open houses, and formal debates. Teachers are learning ways to invite feedback from the audience during these events. This includes involving students in welcoming audience members by describing the learning they are about to see, and then after their presentations, inviting the audience to respond. Responses give students feedback on and acknowledgment for what they have learned.

Student-parent conferences

Student-parent conferences are a time for students to share their learning with their parents. Teachers help students prepare to conduct student-parent conferences, whether they are going to take place at home or at school. There is an agenda and students have organized evidence of their learning, such as their notebooks, projects, or portfolios. They also choose something to demonstrate, such as a book to read aloud. A discussion is led by the student while the evidence of learning is shared. At the end of the conference, students ask their parents to give them feedback on a prepared response form. Sometimes parents and students will also set goals for future learning.

> Congratulations, Everyone
>
> We saw you at the sharing assembly and would like you to know
>
> - We enjoyed your poetry reading
> - It made us laugh
> - We could hear you at the back
>
> Shane's Mom and Dad

There are many different formats for holding conferences at school. One teacher might ask five students to sign up for each 30-minute period. During that time, they conduct their student-parent conference, and the teacher meets with each family for a few minutes. Another teacher might have as many student-parent conferences as there is space and be available to respond to questions. The choices teachers make concerning the number of student-parent conferences to schedule at one time depends on their purpose, the students' needs, their families' needs, and the teacher's comfort level with the process.

> **Dear Guests**
>
> Welcome to our class. Please let your son or daughter be your guide. She or he will teach you about some of the things we do at school.
>
> 1. With your guide, visit the learning centres in our classroom. Ask lots of questions. Your guide will invite you to participate in some of the activites at each centre.
>
> 2. Your guide is also ready to show you:
>
>   - a portfolio and an Assessment Centre collection
>
>   - work samples and notebooks
>
>   - a favourite library book
>
>   - a favourite computer program
>
>   - the book fair in the library
>
> 3. When you are finished your tour, your guide will ask you to complete a response form. This form will ask you to give two compliments and one wish for your child and his or her learning.
>
> Signed,
> Mrs. Ratcliffe

The following example describes how one school approached student-parent conferences by using "learning centres" or "stations." These conferences were held about two weeks before the end of term.

The number of centres depended on the class and ranged in number from 4 to 12. Students invited their families, and together they moved from centre to centre. Most teachers encouraged families to sign up for one of the two hours scheduled for this event. This helped foster an "open house" atmosphere in which families could spend up to an hour visiting the centres.

At each centre, parents participated in an activity that the student was currently doing in the class. This included activities such as building complex patterns using pattern blocks, solving equations, using frames to write poems, reading a book, taking apart something in the Deconstruction Centre, or looking through the student's portfolio in the Assessment Centre.

Teachers posted signs for families that explained some of the key ways the activities related to the curriculum goals and suggested some questions families might want to ask their children. Students were ready to explain what the centre was about, show other work related to the centre activities, and answer their families' questions. As they arrived, guests were given a note that acted as an agenda explaining what would happen during the visit.

Student-parent conferences are a valuable part of communicating about learning, but they do not replace conferences that include the teacher. When evaluation is involved, it is important to have the person who is responsible for evaluation (the teacher) present. This is best done through student-parent-teacher conferences (see Chapter 10).

Dear Parents,

It is helpful for your child to have your comments about his or her learning at the conclusion of math night. When we know we have done something right, we feel good about ourselves. We accept challenges more readily and enthusiastically, and learning becomes easier. In the space below, please give your son or daughter two specific compliments and one wish.

Thank You

Two compliments for: Kayla

• The way you are learning to do math and that you love it.
• That you are always happy after school. You love to learn.

One Wish:

That you continue to love learning and you aren't afraid to ask questions and figure out new ways to solve problems.

From: Mommy and Daddy

Audiences Respond with Feedback

Every time students share their learning with parents or another audience, it is a good idea to invite the audience to respond. Anyone whose opinion the student values can be an audience and provide feedback to support learning. This creates an opportunity for deepening the relationship between student and audience by enhancing the understanding and appreciation of the young person's efforts. Feedback can be as simple as a form that asks the reader to notice something positive about the learning, or additionally, to ask a question, give some advice, or suggest an improvement.

The teacher invites feedback

Whenever we invite students to communicate about their learning to others, it is important to follow up to find out whether it was successful for the students and for the audience. Even with the best of intentions, mistakes are made. We need to know what is working and what is not so that we can continue to improve on our learning path.

Ask students and parents what worked and what did not. Be careful what you ask for. Asking for one or two compliments and one piece of advice is often more than enough. Consider keeping surveys anonymous so students and parents will feel more comfortable expressing their thoughts. Let students and parents know what was said by posting a summary of the comments on the class website, or ask students to include it in the next class newsletter home.

Math Night Survey

Dear Students and Parents:

Feedback is essential for learning - we need to know what worked (do more of) and what did not (do less of). Please help us learn to do a better job by responding to this survey. You do not need to sign it, but please send the completed survey back to the school secretary, so it can be put in the collection box in the office.

Thank you.

What are two compliments you have about Math Night?

We could see the growth in our son's work and confidence. We were pleased to see the variety of his math work. I especially liked that he felt in control. He was proud to show his achievements. I also liked his "agenda". He had a specific order to his work. He was well prepared.

Is there anything you'd like to see or do next time?

It is important for our son to show his learning, but we also want to know what you think. Will you be a part of our report card conference next month? Last year the teacher had lots of conferences at one time, and we didn't get a chance to find out what she thought. After our conference this year, can we sign up if we need to talk to you?

Adapted from Politano and Davies, *Multi-Age and More*, 107

Finding Your Way

When we involve students in communicating about their learning, we are inviting them and their parents to have thoughtful conversations with us and with each other about learning. There is no one *right* or *best* way to do this. Select the method or combination of methods that work for you, your students, and their families in your school community.

❝ *It is good to have an end to journey towards, but it is the journey that matters in the end.* **❞**

Ursula Le Guin

Guiding Our Own Learning

Record your ideas about your current communication practices. Reflect on the following:
- How do you currently communicate with others about student learning?
- How are students involved?
- How could you increase student involvement?
- What kind of balance is best for the students with whom you work?
- Do your students need to be doing more? How could you simplify the process so they can do more?

With a group of colleagues, share ideas about what works. Gather samples. Talk through simple ways to increase student involvement. Recreate your communication plan.

Guiding the Learning of Students

Begin increasing the involvement of students in communicating their learning journey – their evidence of learning – to others. Consider:
1. Dividing up bulletin board space so students each have their own personal display area – when students display their own work, they attach a note that explains why the work sample was selected and what they want the audience to notice about their work.
2. Having students find proof of their learning to share with others, such as:
   - most improved piece of work
   - piece of work most in need of editing
   - piece of work that required the most perseverance
3. Inviting feedback with attached notes, such as: *As you look at my work, please notice…*
4. Initiating a simple four-pocket portfolio, digital or analogue, that highlights the evidence students have created in relation to the course or a subject area's learning destination.

Evaluating and Reporting

When we give grades or comments that try for objectivity or impersonality or general validity, we are very likely – not to put too fine a point on it – to be telling lies.

Peter Elbow

Evaluation and reporting occur at the point in the classroom assessment cycle when the learning pauses, and the evidence is organized and evaluated by comparing it to the standards and outcomes expected the students needed to learn. Then, the results of the evaluation are shared, usually in a report card. The foundation for evaluating and reporting is put in place when the teacher develops the descriptions of learning (Chapter 3), describes what success looks like for students (Chapter 4), and thinks through the evidence that will be needed (Chapter 5). Students are further prepared when they engage in the process of learning through assessment (Chapters 6 & 7) and when they collect evidence and communicate their ongoing learning to others (Chapters 8 & 9).

When it is time to evaluate, teachers revisit those same descriptions of what was to be learned, and review the evidence students have organized, as well as evidence teachers have collected, and then use their professional judgment to make their evaluation. They review their judgment and evidence with students and their parents, and report using the required format. Evaluating and reporting are straightforward last steps in an assessment process that begins much earlier.

Working Together

Evaluating and reporting requires professional judgment in response to the following four issues:

1. What does the student know, what is she or he able to do, and what can she or he articulate?
2. What areas require further attention or development?
3. In what ways can the student's learning be supported?
4. How is the student progressing in relation to the standards or development for students in a similar age range?

Teachers, students, and parents each have a role in the evaluating and reporting process. Students do the learning and along the way, create the evidence of learning. In preparation for evaluation and reporting, they organize the evidence and summarize their strengths, needs, and plans. They present the evidence to account for their learning and listen to feedback. Then, they set goals for future learning.

Parents participate by listening, watching, asking questions, and making sense of the evidence. They interpret the evidence and the accompanying self-assessments that students present, as well as the commentary the teacher gives. To this, they add their own observations of their son or daughter as a learner.

Teachers, because it is their professional responsibility, are the final arbitrators and evaluators of the work. They assist students to communicate their learning to parents, and they make themselves available to discuss how they have evaluated the student's work, as well as ways that student learning could be better supported.

A Subjective Process

The evaluating and reporting process includes: evaluating the evidence, involving students and parents in reviewing the evidence, summarizing strengths and areas needing improvement, and finalizing the report. Teachers' professional lives might be simpler if evaluating and reporting could be tidy and objective, but the process of evaluation is inherently subjective. The more reliable and valid the evidence collected and the longer period of time over which it is collected, the more confidence everyone can have in the evaluation. Also, when students and their parents are engaged in reviewing the evidence and affirming whether or not the evaluation makes sense, sound judgments are more likely. Teachers need to report reliable and valid professional judgment. By looking for patterns and trends over time, based on multiple sources (triangulation) of reliable and valid evidence, the teacher can report in a professional manner.

> **Taking care...**
>
> In evaluation, teachers must be especially careful when working with numbers from performance scales and rubrics. Totalling scores from rubrics and averaging them with other kinds of numbers is like adding mangoes, potatoes, apples and trees. The process does not make mathematical sense.

Evaluating the Evidence

Evaluation is a process of looking at all the evidence, comparing it to the description and samples of quality, and asking: *Did this student learn what was to be learned? How well?* When we evaluate, we determine the worth or value of the evidence – we appraise it with respect to excellence or merit. Simply totaling the grades in our record book means that important evidence may not be considered. To evaluate well, we should look at *all* the evidence – observations, products, and conversations. We can then use this evidence to determine whether the student has met the widely-held expectations for his or her age.

Triangulation of evidence – looking at evidence from three different sources – is essential because it puts single pieces of evidence into context. As a judge in a court of law must examine all the evidence in light of the legal statutes, teachers must look at all the evidence in light of that which must be learned given outcomes, standards, or expectations. We must consider the entire range of indicators – the evidence students have collected, the self-assessments they have made, our observations, criteria-based assessments attached to projects or assignments, performance grids, rubric scores, and grades from projects and tests.

Three-Way Conference Goal Sheet

Name:_____ Date: _____

Goals I have chosen to work on this year:

Goal 1: improve on home work in math – fewer than 5 wrong

Goal 2: improve on writing skills – write at least 5 writing pieces

Student Will:	Parent Will:	Teacher Will:
show homework to mom. Slow down in math. Ask for help.	Goal 1. a. check homework b. quiz on math facts Goal 2. a. look over writing pieces b. make suggestions	Correct the math in a timely fashion. Give assistance. Set clear expectations for written pieces.

Available as a reproducible at connect2learning.com

Reporting

Reporting used to be a special event that happened only at set times in a year. Now it is an ongoing process that involves students, parents, and teachers in examining and making sense of a student's learning. Every time students speak with their parents about learning, they are reporting. That is, whenever they take home a sample of their work and discuss it, or invite parents to a portfolio afternoon to look at their work or to participate in a student-parent-teacher conference, they are reporting.

Formal evaluating and reporting is usually required by legislation or policy and is a process of looking at the evidence, having conversations and conferences about what the evidence means, and keeping a written record of the conversation for the learner's permanent file.

Increasingly, teachers are involving students in the conferencing and reporting process and inviting them and their parents to be part of student-parent-teacher conferences. The purpose of these conferences is to look at the evidence, highlight strengths, discuss areas needing improvement, and set goals during the reporting period.

Mid-Term Informal Report

By:_____

My personal goal for this term was:

_____

_____

_____

Please notice how I:
- have achieved my goal.
- am working on my goal.
- am thinking about starting to work on my goal.

You can know this because:

_____

_____

Parent(s)' Comments:

_____

_____

_____

Parent(s)' Signature: _____

Teacher's Signature: _____

Date: _____

The following accounts illustrate how four teachers are using the reporting process with their primary, intermediate and secondary classes.

Mrs. H has created observation charts for her early primary class that details what she needs to be teaching and observing in the core subject areas.

When reporting time nears, she has students organize their evidence, collect samples for their progress portfolios, and do self-reports. In their self-reports, students record their strengths, areas needing improvement, and goals. They rehearse what they are going to say to their parents. Parents respond with two compliments and one wish. Mrs. H summarizes the evidence on an observation chart, writes a draft report, and shares both her report and the child's self-report with the parents. During their student-parent-teacher conference, they all review the strengths and areas needing improvement. The student leads the conference and shares the progress portfolio, telling what she or he learned. Mrs. H shares the draft report. Together, student, parents, and teacher set goals and discuss support for learning. Once the conference is over, Mrs. H finalizes the one-page narrative report that summarizes the conference discussion. She reads it to the student, checking to see if anything is missing or incorrect. One copy is filed and one is sent home with an invitation for parents to get in touch if there are any remaining questions or concerns. (See the Primary Progress Report on the following page.)

Mr. M has his Grade 7 students organize their evidence, collect samples for their progress portfolios, and do self-reports. In their self-reports, students record their strengths, areas needing improvement, and goals. Mr. M prepares a draft report and shares this and the child's self-report with the parents. Parents are also invited to review the evidence and do a report for their child, highlighting strengths, areas needing improvement, and possible goals. During their student-parent-teacher conference, they review the strengths and areas needing improvement, and set goals. Once the conference is over and the written report is finalized, one copy is filed and one sent home. As part of the follow-up, Mr. M debriefs the process with students, and parents are invited to request a separate parent-teacher conference should they need one. Mr. M gets very few requests for follow-up conferences.

Ms. D teaches high school Social Studies. At mid-term, students fill out a reflection sheet identifying their strengths and areas needing improvement. When they meet, students show her evidence of their learning to date and they set goals. Then, at semester end, the students do a reflective final report where they describe their evidence, showing that they have met the course outcomes, and organize it into a four-pocket portfolio. They meet with Ms. D and present the evidence of learning. Then she assigns percentage grades.

Mr. L follows a similar process in his senior level Mathematics classes. The portfolio of evidence shows proof of learning beyond tests, quizzes and assignments. It is valued as 20% of the final grade.

ELEMENTARY SCHOOL
SCHOOL DISTRICT # ___ (___)
PRIMARY PROGRESS REPORT

> **Student: C**
> **Reporting Period: November to March**
> **Teacher: Grade: 2**

This report describes your child's progress in relation to the curriculum in intellectual, social, human and career development.

Introduction:
____ is a conscientious and capable student who celebrates her many successes with pride. She loves to help and often offers positive, creative suggestions to resolve differences. Her pursuit of excellence has resulted in adopting a reflective approach to her learning with deep understandings and an appreciation for the importance of details. Highlights of her personal focus this term were:
• reading a two voice poem with a classmate at a sharing assembly using excellent presentational skills;
• persevering to write a complete storyline involving complex plot structures; and
• learning new technology so she can publish her writing.

In addition, she has worked hard to successfully achieve the following goals from last term:
• To use capital letters at the beginning of sentences more often;
• To spell verb endings like ed and ing (jumped, liking); and
• To increase the speed of computing math facts; and
Personal Goal: To learn how to do harder subtraction wheels.

Strengths/Accomplishments:
• She reads chapter books with fluency and improving expression (Red Alert);
• She uses a selection of strategies to read unknown words including skip reading, blending, framing, picture clues and predicting;
• She reads for a purpose, researches a topic, and applies these skills to write key words to describe the appearance of a dinosaur;
• She can give the main elements of a complex story plot including title, illustrator, author, characters, main events, problem and solution;
• She is developing skills in interpreting a character profile through the creation of character voices;
• She writes longer sequentially developed stories involving a beginning with setting and character introductions, more relevant supportive details and descriptive language, conversations, a description of events leading to a main climactic problem, and a simple ending;
• She is able to complete the grammar and word study activities with increasing ease;
• She can compare and contrast story elements of more than one title by the same author;
• She can give the main elements of a story including title, illustrator, author, characters, main events, problem and solution;
• Her personal spelling demonstrates a working knowledge of consonants, blends, short vowels, some long vowels with silent e, some vowel partners and some familiar words;
• She can add and subtract numbers to 20 with reasonable speed and accuracy;
• She can give the place value of numbers to 999 in terms of hundreds, tens, and ones and expanded notation (4 hundreds, 7 tens and 9 ones = 400 + 70 + 9 = 479);
• She is learning to add with regrouping using an algorithm (278 + 106);
• She can independently skip count using more complex number patterns (by hundreds: 341, 441, 541);
• She can independently solve mathematical problems using critical, logical and creative thinking skills;
• She can add and subtract three digit numbers without regrouping; and
• She is developing dancing, skating, and fitness skills to enhance endurance and balance.

Areas Requiring Further Attention or Development:
I have no concerns regarding ____'s academic and personal development at this time.

Goals and Support for Learning:
Goals:
• To write in different genres; and
• To read over her written drafts to edit familiar spelling patterns, especially word endings (stopping, stopped), capitalization and punctuation.
Support for learning:
Teacher will underline errors in capitalization, punctuation and common spellings/patterns to edit.
____ is encouraged to:
• read from different genres from other countries to develop a repertoire of plot structures; and
• re-read her written drafts and check for spelling, capitalization and punctuation errors.
Her parents can help her to edit her personal writings at home.

Summary
____ is making excellent progress in all areas of her academic and personal development. She easily meets the widely-held expectations for her age at this time and reads and writes beyond grade-level. She is to be commended on her significant achievements and outstanding efforts.

Teacher _____   Principal _____

Involving Students

Teachers are seeing the benefits of showing students their reports before they go home and of asking questions, such as: *Does this make sense? Does it reflect your learning? Is it fair? Am I missing anything?* This increases the validity of our evaluation because we add the student's perspective to the range of information we have to work with. When students understand their reports, they can explain them to their parents.

> **What students say...**
>
> "I think the conference was good because it gives my parents a really good idea of how I am doing at school."
>
> "I liked it because my Mom got to have a chance to tell my teacher what I am good at. Also I like it because I could tell both my Mom and my teacher what I need to have help on and more stuff."
>
> "I really liked the conference because I got to show my mom lots of stuff that I was doing and because me and Ms. R. made a goal for me, which was to speak up more and be part of the conversation. And I think I'm doing really good at that."

Involving Parents

Keeping track of how their children are doing at school is a challenge for most parents. In a student-and-parent-involved evaluation and reporting process, parents have an opportunity to take part in reviewing the evidence, listening to their son or daughter talk about their strengths and areas needing improvement, helping to set goals for future learning, and identifying plans for supporting the student's learning.

In addition to listening to their child and looking at the evidence, parents need opportunities to listen to the teacher and to have the teacher respond to any questions they may have about their child's learning. After the conference and reporting process is completed, teachers can invite parents to get in touch about any remaining concerns or questions that have arisen about their son's or daughter's learning. Some teachers send home a follow-up survey to invite parents to give feedback about the process.

> **What parents say...**
>
> "I think it helps the child to know that all parties are working together to help them with their progress."
>
> "With three-way conferencing I seem to get a better feel of where my children's strengths and weaknesses are and suggestions on how to work with him. I get a better idea of what is expected of a student of that level."
>
> "I think the conferences are an essential part of reporting. A report card cannot possibly provide all the information available. The opportunity for the student is invaluable."

Compensating for the Compulsory

For many teachers and administrators, the need to work within the reporting guidelines and to support student learning seem contradictory. Bibby and Posterski (1992), in their book *Teen Trends: A Nation in Motion*, used the phrase "compensating for the compulsory" to describe ways to make things work better while living within the rules.

While some teachers are able to report using narrative or anecdotal reports, others must use report card symbols or specific descriptors that summarize the learning. This is one area where teachers find themselves compensating for the compulsory. Many years ago, Kohn (1999) argued that traditional grades are likely to lead to three separate results: less impressive learning, less interest in learning, and less desire for challenging learning. He recommends that if teachers have to give grades, they give as few as possible. Grades get in the way of student learning – so, the best teachers "compensate for the compulsory." Harlen and Deakin-Crick (2003) summarized the research related to motivation, testing and learning, and have come to similar conclusions.

> ### What teachers say...
>
> "During a student-parent-teacher conference... you can show parents what the students can do and discuss this with them. You can find out what individual parents want to know about their child in terms of assessment and reporting. This means less work, as I hold the conference before I write the report card... there are no surprises for the parents and I have an individual report tailored for each student."
>
> "For middle school students there is always a genuine sense of closure and satisfaction about the whole process. There are no loose ends. Student-parent-teacher conferences are the best way to instill a sense of student responsibility for their own learning."
>
> "When the five-year-olds in our program share their progress folios with their families in three-way conferences by showing the work they have done on their goals, it's an amazing learning, teaching, and assessment opportunity all rolled into one."

As teachers, we can't rewrite the regulations that govern reporting, but we can look at them and think about how best to work within them on behalf of student learning. Where jurisdictions still require teachers to report using grades, scores, symbols, numbers or percentages, more and more teachers are talking with students about what counts in their learning, sharing information about how a grade is arrived at before the end of the term, and involving them in the conferencing and reporting process. This helps make the scores a little more useful and better understood. Here is how three teachers report using narratives or descriptions of quality for their report card symbols.

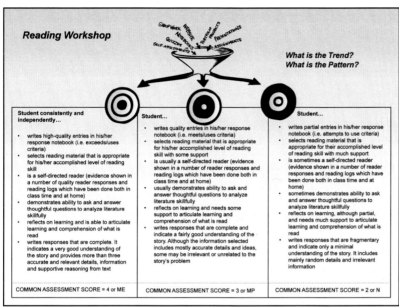

Reading Workshop

GROUP WORK, WEBSITE, NOTEBOOKS, PORTFOLIO, PRESENTATIONS, SELF-ASSESSMENTS, QUIZZES, ASSIGNMENTS

What is the Trend?
What is the Pattern?

Student consistently and independently...	Student...	Student...
• writes high-quality entries in his/her response notebook (i.e. exceeds/uses criteria) • selects reading material that is appropriate for his/her accomplished level of reading skill • is a self-directed reader (evidence shown in a number of quality reader responses and reading logs which have been done both in class time and at home) • demonstrates ability to ask and answer thoughtful questions to analyze literature skillfully • reflects on learning and is able to articulate learning and comprehension of what is read • writes responses that are complete. It indicates a very good understanding of the story and provides more than three accurate and relevant details, information and supportive reasoning from text	• writes quality entries in his/her response notebook (i.e. meets/uses criteria) • selects reading material that is appropriate for his/her accomplished level of reading skill with some support • is usually a self-directed reader (evidence shown in a number of reader responses and reading logs which have been done both in class time and at home) • usually demonstrates ability to ask and answer thoughtful questions to analyze literature skillfully • reflects on learning and needs some support to articulate learning and comprehension of what is read • writes responses that are complete and indicate a fairly good understanding of the story. Although the information selected includes mostly accurate details and ideas, some may be irrelevant or unrelated to the story's problem	• writes partial entries in his/her response notebook (i.e. attempts to use criteria) • selects reading material that is appropriate for their accomplished level of reading skill with much support • is sometimes a self-directed reader (evidence shown in a number of reader responses and reading logs which have been done both in class time and at home) • sometimes demonstrates ability to ask and answer thoughtful questions to analyze literature skillfully • reflects on learning, although partial, and needs much support to articulate learning and comprehension of what is read • writes responses that are fragmentary and indicate only a minimal understanding of the story. It includes mainly random details and irrelevant information
COMMON ASSESSMENT SCORE = 4 or ME	COMMON ASSESSMENT SCORE = 3 or MP	COMMON ASSESSMENT SCORE = 2 or N

With thanks to Cresta McIntosh, Hawaii

Ms. C teaches a fifth-year course to teachers finishing the last year of their degree. She provides students with the course outcomes and a description of each letter grade. She sets criteria for major assignments with the students. At the end of the course, there is a student-teacher conference so students can present to her their evidence of learning in relation to the course outcomes. She reviews all the evidence and uses the description of letter grades to determine students' final grades in the course.

Ms. G teaches Grade 9 English. She has identified what she needs students to learn, the evidence that she will be collecting, and, since she is required to give students letter grades of *A, B, C+,* or *C,* she has described what the learning and evidence look like at each level. Early in the term, she shared these descriptions with students and their parents. Prior to reporting, students organize their evidence into portfolios and review it, to ensure that it includes everything they need to substantiate their grades. Ms. G reviews the student evidence, including the grades she recorded and her own observations, and evaluates the learning. The student is assigned the letter grade that matches the evidence. Each student receives a copy of Ms. G's evaluation. Parents are invited to come to the school for a student-parent conference to view the evidence before the reports are prepared. Once the reports are sent home, parents are invited to call Ms. G if they need to ask any questions about the evaluation or the report, or to sign up for a conference.

Mr. W must report using percentages. He has defined what it means to be a successful student in Biology 11. Both he and his students collect evidence of learning. At the end of the term, Mr. W based 40% of the final grade on evidence collected in relation to the definition of quality titled, 'Being a Scientist.' During the term students select the best evidence they have that they are 'being a scientist' and then, toward the end of the term, make their final selections. They select 2 – 3 pieces of work in each of the five categories of 'Being a Scientist' and put it in a folder. The remaining 60% is based on grades, scores, observations, and interview notes that Mr. W has collected over the term from projects, tests and exams.

Being a Scientist in Biology 11		
Learning Destination	**Evidence of Learning could include:**	**My Evidence of Learning:**
I understand and apply the scientific concepts being studied. I understand and apply the scientific processes being studied. I ask and answer questions about the world. I articulate clear understandings of the scientific process. I make connections to other concepts, to other situations and to life.	Graphic organizers Lab reports Presentations Notes from group work Experiment demonstrations Self- and peer assessments Reading summaries and reflections Video sequences Research projects Tests, quizzes, tasks	

Common Elements

As teachers, you will need to figure out which processes of evaluation and reporting will work for you, your students, and their parents, in your given situation. It may help to consider some of the examples of processes presented in this chapter. These teachers:

- worked within the legal requirements for reporting in their schools and districts

- developed an assessment plan that summarized the learning destination and the evidence of learning, and collected samples to illustrate quality

- developed a description of achievement

- involved students in the classroom assessment process

- collected samples of growth over time

- involved students in collecting and organizing the evidence

- spent time examining the evidence and doing their own evaluation

- checked with students to ensure the teacher's evaluation of their work made sense

- asked parents to review the evidence and invited them to also do a "report" from their perspective

- met with each student and her or his parents to discuss strengths, areas needing improvement, and goals

- told parents whether or not their child's learning was in the "safety zone" or whether intervention was needed

- finalized the report after conversations with participants

- put a copy in the student's permanent file

When you make your plans for evaluating and reporting, take the time to be sure you know what rules and regulations govern these procedures in your school. Ask at the district or province/state level. Don't accept someone else's interpretation of the rules. Become an expert on exactly what you are responsible for, so that you can figure out the best way to use the evaluation and reporting process to support student learning. It is well worth taking this time. You might want to read Herbst and Davies's books *Grading, Reporting, and Professional Judgment in Elementary Classrooms* (2016) or *A Fresh Look at Grading and Reporting in High Schools* (2014) for a more complete step-by-step description of the reporting process. As Mary Jane Drummond (1994) explains, "The process of assessing children's learning – by looking closely at it and striving to understand it – is the only certain safeguard against children's failure, the only certain guarantee of children's progress and development." The idea of looking closely at student work has fueled many powerful initiatives, including building visual continua and moderation of student work. Researchers exploring moderation have documented its positive impact on teacher practice (Adie and Willis 2016; Daugherty 2010; Wyatt-Smith and Klenowski 2008).

A railroad worker in St. Louis accidentally moved a small piece of track three inches. The train on that track was supposed to go to Newark, but ended up in New Orleans, 1300 miles away. Any change – even a tiny one – in your direction today will make a significant difference hundreds of miles down the road.

Stephen Covey

Guiding Our Own Learning

Begin planning for your reporting process:
- Search out copies of relevant documents and regulations with regards to reporting. Be clear about what you must do.
- Record any definitions currently in place for summative symbols, such as grades or numbers.
- Think about how to expand the definitions so as to include more information about learning and the qualities likely to be apparent in the evidence if students have learned well.
- Create your own description of achievement for one course or subject area, modeled after the examples in this chapter. Ask a colleague to review it. When you are confident that it accurately describes what students are expected to know, be able to do and articulate, share it with one group of students. Try it out. Modify and refine it until you are comfortable enough to share it with other students and their parents.

Guiding the Learning of Students

As you prepare students to self-assess their way to success, share the description of achievement for one term with them. Ask students to build a list of possible evidence with you. Record all their ideas. Add your own.

Periodically ask students to collect evidence of their learning in relation to the description of achievement. Then, as reporting time draws near, have them finalize their collection of evidence and present it to you, along with a self-report that describes how well they have learned and what they need to learn next. Remind students to attach proof – a piece of evidence – to each statement they make. When students are ready, have them present their evidence to you, and if they are prepared, to others.

This one change, from *teachers* being accountable to *students* being accountable, can make a huge difference in who is seen as responsible for learning. Students need to assume ownership for their learning.

Learning by Ourselves and With Others

" Much of the process of education consists of being able to distance oneself in some way from what one knows by being able to reflect on one's own knowledge. "

Jerome Bruner

Making assessment work in support of student learning is an ongoing task for teachers. Keeping ourselves learning and on track can be a challenge in our busy lives. One approach teachers find helpful is to be part of a group of people learning together. These days, most educators refer to these groups as *learning teams* or *professional learning communities*. My favourite term is *learning circles* – places where people learn from each other.

When we learn together, we share experiences that help us understand our thinking. This helps us grow and develop at our own pace. Sometimes *belonging* means following structured protocols to deepen our learning in certain, deliberate ways. Other times, the learning circle's journey is more evolutionary. As members of a learning group, we can access the support we need to take risks, or to prevent us from leaping without a parachute.

Your Learning Circle

You probably already belong to more than one learning circle. Some may be formally established and part of your job. Others are adopted or created by you. Some will last for months and others, for years.

We are learning all the time – by talking with others about what we are trying, by sharing books that are helping us learn, or by calling someone to share a success or get advice. We know that sometimes we need to learn by ourselves and sometimes, we need input from others. At those times, friends and colleagues can help us realize what we know and what we want to learn more about.

Some books designed to complement this book are the Knowing What Counts series: *Setting and Using Criteria; Self-Assessment and Goal Setting; Collecting Evidence and Portfolios: Engaging Students in Pedagogical Documentation;* and *Conferencing and Reporting.*

Teachers as Learners and Researchers

To be effective, learning circles must be implemented in ways that are respectful of adults as learners. When participants are invited to be involved and when they choose what and how they are going to learn, the power of their learning can be astonishing.

Sometimes potential participants choose not to accept the invitation to learn about and research classroom assessment. It may be that they are not ready to explore this process at their stage of development. At the same time, they might offer insights and helpful suggestions on ways to create a learning circle that is more accessible and supportive to all learners. Be willing to listen and plan accordingly.

We need to remember that we all learn in different ways and at different times. When we treat our colleagues with as much respect as we try to treat our students, and when we provide a variety of learning experiences, we begin to build a safe learning environment. Ask colleagues for ideas about what kind of support they need to meet their professional goals. Unless adults feel safe enough to take the risks necessary to learn, change will never happen. Go slowly. A safe destination can be achieved by many varied routes.

You might want to recommend your school leadership team read *Leading the Way to Assessment For Learning: A Practical Guide* (Davies, Herbst, and Parrott Reynolds 2012).

Guidelines to Consider

Here are some guidelines that might help you form a learning circle:

- Start small.
- Get organized together.
- Share responsibility.

Start small

Begin with a few people you think might be interested in learning more about supporting student learning through assessment. Draw up a list of people and call them to arrange a time to get together for a first gathering. Even one person is a good start; over time you will find others to join you. Your learning circle can begin by sharing favourite assessment resources or by having participants give their own accounts of assessment. Invite participants to describe incidents that caused them to become interested in improving classroom assessment for their students. Listen to each other and ask questions. Find out if there are common threads of experience. Look for shared interests within the field of classroom assessment.

Get organized together

Acting as a leader for the first gathering, explain your vision for the group. Briefly touch on the following issues:

- Name the reasons for starting a group.
- Decide what the group might do or accomplish.
- Consider whether it will be more like a book club, a time to share successful classroom assessment ideas, or a combination of both.
- Discuss whether to use a book (this one or another) as a guide.
- Develop a plan for where and how often the group might meet.
- Talk about how each gathering could proceed and be organized.

After you share your ideas, ask participants to share theirs. Feel your way, through conversation, toward a final agreement on these issues. Avoid being overly ambitious. The more obligations you put on yourselves, the less likely they will be fulfilled. Consider meeting once a month rather than biweekly. Consider skipping particularly busy months.

Share responsibility

Each meeting is conducted by someone who's been designated in advance: e.g., the group leader, the person hosting the meeting, or a volunteer. The organizer sends reminders about upcoming meetings and devises alternative plans if needed. A facilitator keeps the meeting on track by ensuring that everyone has a chance to contribute and an agreed-upon structure is followed.

Advice from Learning Circles

+ Be respectful of each other.

+ Agree that being a professional means adapting, not adopting, new ideas.

+ Agree that there are lots of right ways to teach, assess, and learn.

+ Ask thoughtful questions.

+ Welcome all points of view.

+ Limit the frequency and length of meetings.

+ Agree how participants will take turns talking.

+ Agree to give each speaker undivided attention without interrupting.

+ Agree to refrain from giving advice or ideas unless the speaker requests them.

+ Agree that conversations at the meeting should not be repeated elsewhere unless permission is granted by the person sharing the story.

Having '*Making Classroom Assessment Work*' Conversations

We can learn by ourselves, with our grade or department level colleagues, with a school faculty, across a family of schools, or across a large professional group of educators.

Learning by ourselves and with colleagues

This book is designed to deepen your understanding of classroom assessment, through reading and through application of the ideas found in the *Guiding Your Own Learning* activities at the end of each chapter.

Consider introducing your colleagues to *Making Classroom Assessment Work* (Fourth Edition) using the structured conversation on the following page.

You might also want to access the Academy at connect2learning.com to find more online resources.

Learning with our department or grade-level colleagues

Creating a learning circle of your grade level or department colleagues and sharing your work related to classroom assessment will help you benefit from your colleague's expertise and give you someone with whom to try out your ideas. Consider using suggestions from other resources, such as *Quality Assessment in High Schools: Accounts From Teachers* (2013), a book full of practical examples from educators across Canada and the US and *7 Actions of Assessment for Learning: Accounts From Elementary Classrooms* (2020) or *A Fresh Look at Grading and Reporting in High Schools* (2014) and *Grading, Reporting, and Professional Judgment in Elementary Classrooms* (2016).

Learning Goal:

The purpose of this session is to focus participants on the elements of comprehensive classroom assessment and give them an overview of the entire process. It is also designed to help participants formulate questions to guide their own reading of the text and their conversations with one another.

Materials:

Making Classroom Assessment Work for each participant. Chart paper for sharing and listing of questions.

Getting Started:

1. Explain that the purpose of classroom assessment is to support student learning and also, to communicate evidence of that learning to others.
2. Acknowledge that we all have different ways and use different strategies to assess student learning. We use the assessment information we gather to support the different learning needs of students.
3. Note that one of our jobs as professionals is to learn about assessment and thoughtfully select a set of ideas and strategies that make sense for the students in our school community.
4. Then, number off the participants from one to ten and ask them to read one chapter in *Making Classroom Assessment Work*, so that each chapter is read by one or more people.
5. As they read, the task of participants is to note two or three ideas that capture the message of the chapter, and to form one question about it. If participants finish early, encourage them to browse the other chapters.
6. Arrange participants into "expert groups" (one's together, two's together and so on) to discuss their findings and questions.
7. Rearrange participants into groups of one to ten. Invite them to talk about the big picture of classroom assessment. Ask one person to record questions that arise.

Debriefing the Learning:

As a large group, record the questions that have arisen. Invite participants to use these questions to focus subsequent learning conversations.

Taking Action:

Choose one or more:
• Encourage participants to read the rest of the book and generate more questions.
• Invite participants to work independently on the Guiding Your Own Learning at the end of each chapter.
• Decide the next steps in exploring classroom assessment.

Extending the Learning:

If participants are interested in learning more about specific ways to involve students in assessment, consider extending the learning by using one or more of the 18 learning conversations found in the *Facilitator's Guide to Classroom Assessment K-12* (a multimedia resource), available at http://connect2learning.com/store/cp

Learning across our school

Some schools have chosen to use *Making Classroom Assessment Work* (Fourth Edition) as an applied book study, where educators work by themselves, with grade-level or department colleagues and then across grades or departments, in order to build a comprehensive school-wide approach to classroom assessment. This school-wide dialogue allows teachers to build upon the experiences students have in other classes, thereby building a common language between students, teachers (and over time, parents).

Learning across many schools

In some places, groups of schools have gathered to extend the conversation across buildings, so that families of schools (elementary to middle to secondary) have a common language and set of experiences upon which to build.

Educators who are engaged in professional development as part of a larger jurisdiction, have used a variety of resources, including this book and others to support ongoing learning about classroom assessment through Academy at connect2learning.com.

Remember that learning circles are powerful circles of friends (or soon-to-be friends), learning together. They arise out of common interests and a willingness to share the journey with others. They last as long as they work, coming in and out of existence, as people pose questions and answer them.

> **"**At first they said it couldn't be done but some were doing it. Then they said it could only be done by a few under special conditions, but more were doing it. Then they said, 'Why would you do it any other way?'**"**
>
> *Anonymous*

Final Thoughts

"Everyone does the best they can at any moment in time. No one ever sets out to make a mistake. However, once we know better, we are obligated to do better."

Anonymous

In this new millennium, educators and students are walking a different path from where the roots of education began. Over a hundred years ago, schools were developed to address the problem of how to rank, sort, and group children for their roles in the industrial world. Assessment became a large part of the solution. Now, even though the problem has changed, education continues to employ many of the same old systems.

Today, we are seeking to ensure that each young person leaves his or her family, community, and school prepared to be an independent, self-directed, lifelong learner – a person who will likely have many careers over a lifetime or who will continually be entrepreneurial, responding to new opportunities given the huge societal changes underway. Using strategies from the past – such as more testing, more failure and retention, higher standards, more rewards, greater punishments, and tighter control over students and their learning – is hurting, not helping.

Making classroom assessment work means reframing the conversation from one about ranking and sorting students to one about assessing learning in the context of our students' futures. It means talking with students, parents, and the community and listening to what they say about learning and about assessment. It means involving students and parents, giving choices, and sharing control. When it comes to classroom assessment, solutions can only be found in thoughtful, informed conversation, as we work together on behalf of students and their learning.

Teachers, students, and parents need the flexibility to address individual needs, as well as provide for choice and diversity, in order to support each student's learning. Each individual will find her or his own expression, in the same way that a tune can be sung – beautifully, but in many different ways, by many different singers.

The role of the educator is to equip others with the necessary skills to assess their own learning, and also to model how it can be done. When we show our students the way to value and demonstrate what they have learned, they follow in our footsteps... until ultimately, they will find their own path to a successful lifelong learning journey.

There are many opportunities to evaluate less. We need to start doing so more accurately, fairly, and hopefully than we usually do.

Peter Elbow

Acknowledgements

I am blessed in this life. Children have taught me how they each learn best and how I could, perhaps, be of assistance. Many fine adults, some of whom have been educators, have educated me. This book is evidence of some of that learning.

A book like this arises from many conversations and learning experiences. When I have been able to attribute a specific idea or example to a specific person, I have tried to do so in the text. Even this fails to acknowledge all that others have shared with me. My apologies for this inadequacy and my deep gratitude to all of you – named and unnamed – who have contributed to my learning and teaching, especially colleagues from across Canada, the United States, Australia, Singapore, Germany, Norway, UK, Ireland, Switzerland, Japan, China, India, and New Zealand.

I dedicated the first edition to my parents, Patricia and William Davies. The gift of their love and the examples their lives provided have helped me immensely.

I would also like to thank my husband, Stewart Duncan (1944-2017), and our children and grandchildren, Bambi, Sheena, Mackenzie, Kayla and Dakota. My life is more interesting, more fun, and more fulfilling because of you. Thank you for living this life with me.

Anne

References

Adie, L. and J. Willis. 2016. Making meaning of assessment policy in Australia through teacher assessment conversations. In D. Laveault and L. Allal, (Eds.) *Assessment for Learning: Meeting the Challenge of Implementation* (pp. 35-53). New York: Springer.

Alexander, R. J. 2000. *Culture And Pedagogy: International Comparisons In Primary Education*. Oxford, UK: Blackwell.

Allal, L. 2016. The co-regulation of student learning in an assessment for learning culture. In D. Laveault & L. Allal (Eds.), *Assessment For Learning: Meeting The Challenge Of Implementation*. (pp. 259-273). New York: Springer.

Andrade, H. 2011. *Foreword*. In Gregory, K., Cameron, C., and Davies, A., *Self-Assessment And Goal Setting* (pp. 7-16). Courtenay, BC: Connections Publishing.

Assessment Reform Group. 2006. ARG-ASF Project, Working Papers 1-4. Assessment systems for the future: the place of assessment by teachers. http://k1.ioe.ac.uk/tlrp/arg/ASF.html

Biddle, B. and D. Berliner. 1998. *The Manufactured Crisis*. Don, Mills, ON: Addison-Wesley Publishing Company, Inc.

Black, P. and D. Wiliam. 1998. Inside the black box: Raising standards through classroom assessment. *Phi Delta Kappan* 80, no. 2: 1-20.

Black, P. and D. Wiliam. 1998. Assessment and classroom learning. *Assessment in Education: Principles, Policy and Practice* 5, no.1: 7-75.

Black, P. and D. Wiliam. 2009. Developing the theory of formative assessment. *Educational Assessment. Evaluation and Accountability* 21, no.1: 5-31.

Black, P. and D. Wiliam. 2018. Classroom assessment and pedagogy. *Assessment in Education: Principles, Policy and Practice* 25 no. 6: 551-575, DOI: 10.1080/0969594X.2018.1441807

Boud, D. 2003. *Enhancing Learning through Self-Assessment*. London and New York: RoutledgeFalmer.

Brabeck, M. 2008. Why we need 'translational' research: Putting clinical findings to work in classrooms. *Education Week* 27 no. 38: 28, 36 (May 20, 2008). https://www.edweek.org/ew/articles/2008/05/21/38brabeck.h27.html

Bransford, J.D., A.L. Brown, and R.R. Cocking. 2000. How People Learn : Brain, Mind, Experience, And School (Expanded edition). Washington, DC: National Academy of Sciences: Committee on Developments in the Science of Learning and Committee on Learning Research and Educational Practice.

British Columbia Ministry of Education. 2000. *Primary Program: A Framework for Teaching*. Victoria, BC: Queens' Printer.

Brookhart, S. 2001. Successful students' formative and summative uses of assessment information. *Assessment in Education: Principles, Policy and Practice* 8, no. 21: 153-169.

Bruner, J. 1986. *Actual Minds, Possible Worlds*. Cambridge, MA: Harvard University Press.

Butler, R. 1987. Task-involving and ego-involving properties of evaluation: Effects of different feedback conditions on motivational perceptions, interest and performance. *Journal of Educational Psychology* 79, no. 4: 474-482.

Butler, R. 1988. Enhancing and undermining intrinsic motivation: The effects of task–involving and ego-involving evaluation on interest and performance. *British Journal of Educational Psychology*. 58: 1-14.

Butler, R. and M. Nisan. 1986. Effects of no feedback, task-related comments and grades on intrinsic motivation and performance. *Journal of Educational Psychology* 78, no. 3: 210-216.

Centre for Educational Research and Innovation. 2005. *Formative Assessment: Improving Learning in Secondary Classrooms*. London, UK: OECD Publishing.

Centre for Educational Research and Innovation (CERI). 2007. *Understanding the Brain: Towards a New Learning Science* (Vol. 2). Paris, France: OECD. https://www.oecd.org/education/ceri/understandingthebrainthebirthofale-arningscience.htm

Crooks, T. 1988. The impact of classroom evaluation on students. *Review of Educational Research* 58, no. 4: 438-481.

Csikszentmihalyi, M. 1993. *The Evolving Self: A Psychology for the Millennium*. New York: Harper Collins.

Daugherty, J. 2010. Summative assessment: The role of teachers. In P. Peterson, B. Baker, and B. McGaw (Eds.), *International Encyclopedia of Education* 3: 348-391. Oxford, UK: Elsevier.

Davies, A. 2004. *Finding Proof of Learning in a One-to-One Computing Classroom*. Courtenay, BC: Connections Publishing.

Davies, A., S. Herbst, and B. Parrott Reynolds. 2012. *Leading the Way to Assessment for Learning: A Practical Guide*. Courtenay, BC: Connections Publishing.

Davies, A., S. Herbst, and K. Busick (Eds.) 2013. *Quality Assessment in High Schools: Accounts From Teachers*. Courtenay, BC: Connections Publishing.

Davies, A., S. Herbst, and B. Augusta. 2017. *Collecting Evidence and Portfolios: Engaging Students in Pedagogical Documentation*. Courtenay, BC: Connections Publishing.

Deci, E. and R.M. Ryan. *2002. Handbook of Self-Determination Research*. New York: University of Rochester Press.

Dewey, J. 1933. *How We Think: A Restatement of the Relation of Reflective Thinking To the Educative Process*. Lexington, MA: Heath.

Drummond, M.J. 1994. *Learning to See: Assessment Through Observation*. Markham, ON: Pembroke Publishers.

Dweck, C.S. 2000. *Self-Theories: Their Role in Motivation, Personality and Development*. Philadelphia, PA: The Psychology Press.

Elbow, P. 1986. *Embracing Contraries: Explorations in Learning and Teaching*. New York: Oxford University Press.

Fullan, M. 2001. *Leading in a Culture of Change*. San Francisco, CA: Jossey-Bass Inc.

Gardner, H. 1984. *Frames of Mind: The Theory of Multiple Intelligences*. New York: Basic Books.

Gardner, J. (Ed.). 2005. *Assessment and Learning*. Thousand Oaks, CA: Sage Publications.

Gearhart, M. and S. Wolf. 1995. *Teachers' and Students' Roles in Large-Scale Portfolio Assessment: Providing Evidence of Competency with the Purpose and Processes of Writing (CSE Report 406)*. Los Angeles, CA: UCLA/The National Center for Research on Evaluation, Standards, andStudent Testing. (CRESST).

Gibbs, C. and G. Stobart. 1993. *Assessment: A Teacher's Guide to the Issues*, 2nd Ed. Oxford, UK: Hodder and Stoughton.

Glaude, C. 2005. *Protocols for Professional Learning Conversations*. Courtenay, BC: Connections Publishing.

Gregory, K., C. Cameron, and A. Davies. 2011a. *Knowing What Counts: Setting and Using Criteria*, 2nd Ed. Courtenay, BC: ConnectionsPublishing.

Gregory, K., C. Cameron, and A. Davies. 2011b. *Knowing What Counts: Self-Assessment and Goal Setting*, 2nd Ed. Courtenay, BC: Connections Publishing.

Gregory, K., C. Cameron, and A. Davies. 2011c. *Knowing What Counts: Conferencing and Reporting*, 2nd Ed. Courtenay, BC: Connections Publishing.

Harlen, W. 2006. *The Role Of Teachers In The Assessment Of Learning*. Pamphlet produced by Assessment Systems for the Future project (ASF) Assessment Reform Group, UK. http://k1.ioe.ac.uk/tlrp/arg/images/ Pamphlet%20-%20 role%20of%20teachers.pdf

Harlen, W. and R. Deakin-Crick. 2002. *Testing, Motivation and Learning*. Booklet produced by Assessment Reform Group at University of Cambridge Faculty of Education. http://k1.ioe.ac.uk/tlrp.arg/TML%BOOKLET%20complete.pdf

Harlen, W. and R. Deakin-Crick. 2003. Testing and motivation for learning. *Assessment in Education: Principles, Policy and Practice* 10, no. 2: 169-208.

Hattie, J. 2008. *Visible Learning: A Synthesis of Over 800 Meta-Analyses Relating to Achievement*. New York: Routledge.

Hattie, J. and H. Timperley. 2007. The power of feedback. *Review of Educational Research 77*, no. 1: 81-112.

Hayward, L. 2015. Assessment is learning: The preposition vanishes. *Assessment in Education: Principles, Policy and Practice* 22 no. 1: 27-43.

Henderson, A.T. and N. Berla. (Eds.) 1994. *A New Generation of Evidence: The Family is Critical to Student Achievement*. Washington, DC: National Committee for Citizens in Education.

Herbst, S. and A. Davies. 2014. *A Fresh Look at Grading and Reporting in High Schools*. Courtenay, BC: Connections Publishing.

Herbst, S. and A. Davies. 2016. *Grading, Reporting, and Professional Judgment in Elementary Classrooms*. Courtenay, BC: Connections Publishing.

Hill, M., Ell, F., Grudnoff, L., Haigh, M., Cochran-Smith, M., and Chang, WC. 2017. Assessment for equity: Learning how to use evidence to scaffold learning and improve teaching. *Assessment in Education: Principles, Policy and Practice* 24, no. 2: 185-204.

Hurford, S. 1998. I can see clearly now – student learning profiles. *Primary Leadership* 1, no. 2: 22-29.

Jensen, E. 1998. *Teaching with the Brain in Mind*. Alexandria, VA: ASCD.

Johnston, P.H. 2004. *Choice Words: How Our Language Affects Children's Learning*. Portsmouth, NH: Stenhouse Publishers.

Joslin, G. 2002. *Investigating the Infl uence of Rubric Assessment Practices on the Student's Desire to Learn*. Unpublished manuscript. San Diego State University.

Klenowski, V. and Wyatt-Smith, C. 2014. *Assessment for Education: Standards, Judgement and Moderation*. Thousand Oaks, CA: SAGE Publications Ltd.

Langer, E.J. 1997. *The Power of Mindful Learning.* Reading, MA: Addison-Wesley Publishing Company Inc.

Le Doux, J. 1996. *The Emotional Brain.* New York: Simon and Schuster.

Lincoln, Y. and E. Guba. 1984. *Naturalistic Inquiry.* Beverly Hills, CA: Sage Publications.

Meisels, S., S. Atkins-Burnett, Y. Xue, D.D. Bickel, and S.H. Son. 2003. Creating a system of accountability: The impact of instructional assessment on elementary children's achievement scores. *Educational Policy Analysis Archives,* 11, no. 9. 19 pages. Retrieved September 19, 2004 from http://epaa.asu.edu/epaa/v11n9/

Michaels, S., O'Connor, C., and Resnick, L. 2008. Reasoned participation: Accountable talk in the classroom and in civic life. *Studies in Philosophy and Education* 27, no. 4: 283-297.

Mislevy, R.J. and M.M. Riconscente 2005. *Evidence-Centered Assessment Design: Layers, Structures, And Terminology.* Menlo Park, CA: SRI International Center for Technology in Learning.

National Scientific Council on the Developing Child. 2015. *Supportive Relationships and Active Skill-Building Strengthen the Foundations of Resilience: Working Paper No. 13.* Retrieved from www.developingchild.harvard.edu.

Nye, K. 1999. Open house: Let the kids do it. *Primary Leadership* 2, no. 1: 26-27.

Perrenoud, P. 1998. From formative evaluation to a controlled regulation of learning processes. Towards a wider conceptual field. *Assessment in Education: Principles, Policy and Practice* 5, No. 1: 85-102.

Pert, C. 1999. *Molecules of Emotion: The Science Behind Mind-Body Medicine.* New York: Scribner.

Pinker, S. 1997. *How the Mind Works.* New York: HarperCollins Publisher.

Proschaska, J.O., C. DiClemente, and J. Norcross. 1994. *Changing for Good.* New York: HarperCollins Publishers.

Restak, R. 2003. The New Brain: How the Modern Age is Rewiring Your Mind. New York: St Martin's Press.

Rodriguez, M.C. 2004. The role of classroom assessment in student performance on TIMSS. *Applied Measurement in Education* 17, no. 1: 1-24.

Sadler, D. R. 1989. Formative assessment and the design of instructional systems. *Instructional Science* 16, no. 2: 119-144.

Shepard, L. 2000. The role of assessment in a learning culture. *Educational Researcher* 29, no. 7: 4-14.

Shute, V. 2008. Focus on formative feedback. *Review of Educational Research* 78, no. 1: 13-189. DOI:10.3102/0034654307313795.

Stiggins, R. 2004. *Student-Involved Assessment for Learning*, 4th Ed. Upper Saddle River, NJ: Pearson Prentice Hall.

Stiggins, R. 2007. Assessment through the student's eyes. *Educational Leadership* 64, no. 8: 22-26.

Sueoka, L. 2013. A culture of learning: Building a community of shared learning through student online portfolios. In A. Davies, S. Herbst, and K. Busick (Eds.), *Quality Assessment in High Schools: Accounts From Teachers* (pp. 151-161). Courtenay, BC: Connections Publishing.

Tyler, R. 1949. *Basic Principles of Curriculum and Instruction*. Chicago, IL: University of Chicago Press.

Vygotsky, L.S. 1978. *Mind in Society: the Development of Higher Psychological Processes*. Cambridge, MA: Harvard University Press.

Walters, J., S. Seidel, and H. Gardner. 1994. Children as reflective practitioners. In K.C. Block and J.N. Magnieri, (Eds.), *Creating Powerful Thinking in Teachers and Students*. New York: Harcourt Brace.

Werner, E. and R. Smith. 1992. *Overcoming the Odds: High Risk Children from Birth to Adulthood*. Ithaca, NY: Cornell University Press.

Wiliam, D., C. Lee, C. Harrison, and P. Black. 2004. Teachers developing assessment for learning: Impact on student achievement. *Assessment in Education: Principles Policy and Practice*, 11 no. 1: 49–65.

Wyatt-Smith, C. and Klenowski, V. 2008. Examining how moderation is enacted within an assessment policy reform initiative: You just have to learn how to see, in: 34th International Association for Educational Assessment (IAEA) Annual Conference, 7–12 September 2008, Cambridge, England.

Young, E. 2000. *Enhancing Student Writing by Teaching Self-Assessment Strategies That Incorporate the Criteria of Good Writers*. Submitted in partial fulfillment of requirements for the degree of Doctor of Education to the Department of Educational Psychology, State University of New Jersey, Graduate School of Education, Rutgers.

Appendix A: Reproducibles

You can download digital copies of these reproducibles (see images below) at https://connect2learning.com

Book Conversation Guide

Learning Goal:

This Conversation will focus on the elements of comprehensive classroom assessment. It will help formulate questions to focus further study and introduce the text, *Making Classroom Assessment Work*, 4th Edition.

Materials:

Making Classroom Assessment Work, 4th Edition by Anne Davies for each participant. (Connections Publishing, Courtenay B.C.) https://store.connect2learning.com

Getting Started:

1. Explain that the purpose of classroom assessment is to support learning and also to communicate evidence of that learning to others.

2. Note that we all use different strategies to assess learning. We use that information to support learning in different ways, depending on the needs of students. Our job as professionals is to learn about classroom assessment and to choose the set of assessment ideas and strategies that will best aid us in helping students learn.

3. Number off from 1 to 10. Ask each participant to read one chapter in *Making Classroom Assessment Work*, so that the whole book is read. Ask readers to note two or three ideas that capture the message of the chapter, and to form one question about it. If participants finish their reading early, encourage them to browse through the rest of the book until everyone has finished.

4. Arrange participants in "expert groups" (1s together, 2s together, etc.) to discuss their findings and questions.

5. Rearrange participants in groups of 1 to 10. Invite them to talk about the big picture of classroom assessment. Ask one person to record questions that arise.

Debriefing the Learning:

As a large group, record the questions that have arisen. Invite participants to use these questions to focus future learning.

Taking Action:

Choose one or more:
- Encourage participants to read the rest of the book and generate more questions.
- Invite participants to work independently on end of chapter tasks.
- Decide the next step in exploring classroom assessment.

Extending the Learning:

Choose another book-based conversation at connect2learning.com.

Further Reading

If you've found this book interesting and helpful, you might also like:

1. The Knowing What Counts set of books because they provide the practical "how to" of involving students in assessment (available in English and French).
   - *Setting and Using Criteria*
   - *Self-Assessment and Goal Setting*
   - *Collecting Evidence and Portfolios: Involving Students in Pedagogical Documentation*
   - *Conferencing and Reporting*

2. You might like to read 2 books focusing on accounts from classroom teachers:
   - *7 Actions of Assessment for Learning: Accounts From Elementary Classrooms*
   - *Quality Assessment in High Schools: Accounts From Teachers*

3. You might like to read a book focused on Grading and Reporting for your grade level of interest:
   - *Grading, Reporting and Professional Judgment in Elementary Classrooms*
   - *A Fresh Look at Grading and Reporting in High Schools*

4. If you are a School or System Leader, you might enjoy the companion to this book:
   - *Leading the Way to Assessment for Learning: A Practical Guide*

You can also find many helpful online courses and resources at connect2learning.com

About the Author

Working alongside and encouraging people to achieve their goals - by truly making a difference in the lives of learners - has led to Anne Davies' distinguished and internationally-recognized career in Education Leadership and Assessment.

With extensive classroom and consultation experience with education leaders, Anne uses her depth of knowledge and innovative mindset to help educators realize their own potential for positive impact in the classroom, and beyond.

Anne is the author and co-author of more than 30 books and multimedia resources, including the best seller, *Making Classroom Assessment Work*, now in its fourth edition. She has also published an abundance of chapters and articles, garnering high-profile accolades including the Hilroy Fellowship for outstanding innovation in education, and a nomination for the Canadian Education Association's Whitworth Research Award.

At the core of Anne's learning philosophy is an obligation to honour everyone's abilities and individual methods of expression. Assessment is not about who has 'won the race' - the task at hand is to empower learners, and educators, to effectively use their unique strengths.

These ideas inspire her to continue guiding our education systems - and the individuals responsible for helping learners of all kinds - towards attentive, pragmatic classroom assessment methods.